Accumula 8

STUDENT BOOK

JUMP Math
One Yonge Street, Suite 1014
Toronto, Ontario M5E 1E5
Canada
www.jumpmath.org

Writers: Dr. Anna Klebanov, Saverio Mercurio, Dr. Sohrab Rahbar
Editors: Megan Burns, Liane Tsui, Natalie Francis, Dishpreet Kaur, Jackie Dulson, Janice Dyer, Laura Edlund, Rachelle Redford, Joe Zingrone
Layout and Illustrations: Linh Lam, Fely Guinasao-Fernandes, Sawyer Paul, Marijke Friesen, Ilyana Martinez
Cover Design: Sunday Lek
Cover Photograph: © rorozoa/Freepik.com

ISBN 978-1-77395-300-7

First printing January 2024

Parts of this material were first published in 2015 in AP Book 8.1, US edition (978-1-927457-52-8) and AP Book 8.2, US edition (978-1-927457-53-5).

Printed and bound in Canada

Welcome to JUMP Math!

Entering the world of JUMP Math means believing that every learner has the capacity to be fully numerate and love math.

The **JUMP Math Accumula Student Book** is the companion to the **JUMP Math Accumula** supplementary resource for Grades 1 to 8, which is designed to strengthen foundational math knowledge and prepare all students for success in understanding math problems at grade level. This book provides opportunities for students to consolidate learning by exploring important math concepts through independent practice.

Unique Evidence-Based Approach and Resources

JUMP Math's unique approach, Kindergarten to Grade 8 resources, and professional learning for teachers have been producing positive learning outcomes for children and teachers in classrooms in Canada, the United States, and other countries for over 20 years. Our resources are aligned with the science on how children's brains learn best and have been demonstrated through studies to greatly improve problem solving, computation, and fluency skills. (See our research at **jumpmath.org**.) Our approach is designed to build equity by supporting the full spectrum of learners to achieve success in math.

Confidence Building is Key

JUMP Math begins each grade with review to enable every student to quickly develop the confidence needed to engage deeply with math. Our distinctive incremental approach to learning math concepts gradually increases the level of difficulty for students, empowering them to become motivated, independent problem solvers. Our books are also designed with simple pictures and models to avoid overwhelming learners when introducing new concepts, enabling them to see the deep structure of the math and gain the confidence to solve a wide range of math problems.

About JUMP Math

JUMP Math is a non-profit organization dedicated to helping every child in every classroom develop confidence, understanding, and a love of math. JUMP Math also offers a comprehensive set of classroom resources for students in Kindergarten to Grade 8.

For more information, visit JUMP Math at: www.jumpmath.org.

Contents

1. Multiplication Review

Multiplication is a short form for repeated addition.   Example: $3 \times 5 = \underbrace{5 + 5 + 5}_{\text{add three 5s}}$

1. Write as repeated addition, then calculate.

a) 4×5 b) 5×3 c) 2×4 d) 1×3

$= 5 + 5 + 5 + 5$

$= 20$

2. Write as a product, then calculate.

a) $4 + 4 + 4 + 4 + 4$ b) $5 + 5 + 5$ c) $2 + 2 + 2 + 2$ d) $1 + 1 + 1$

$= 5 \times 4$

$= 20$

3. What do you notice about the answers to 4×5 and 5×4, 5×3 and 3×5,

2×4 and 4×2, and 1×3 and 3×1? _____

Multiplication is **commutative**.   Example: $8 \times 7 = 7 \times 8$

4. Complete the sentence.

a) $9 \times 6 = 54$,   b) $7 \times 6 = 42$,   c) $8 \times 4 = 32$,   d) $12 \times 10 = 120$,

so $\underline{6 \times 9 = 54}$.   so _____.   so _____.   so _____.

You can use multiplication to find the number of items in an array.

 $5 + 5 + 5 = 3 \times 5 = 15$ or    $3 + 3 + 3 + 3 + 3 = 5 \times 3 = 15$

5. Write two multiplication equations to find the number of items in the array.

a)   b)   c) 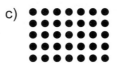   d)

$\underline{3 \times 4 = 12}$ _____   _____   _____

$\underline{4 \times 3 = 12}$ _____   _____   _____

You can multiply 234 × 2 using place values or the standard algorithm.

Place values

2 hundreds + 3 tens + 4 ones

$\underline{\phantom{2 \text{ hundreds} + 3 \text{ tens} + 4} \times 2}$

4 hundreds + 6 tens + 8 ones

= 468

Standard algorithm

	2	3	4
×			2
	4	6	8

6. Multiply using the standard algorithm.

a) 213 × 3

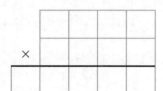

b) 212 × 4

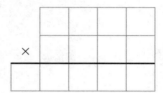

c) 2,301 × 3

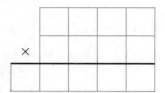

To multiply 218 × 4, you need to regroup.

Place values

  2 hundreds + 1 ten + 8 ones

$\underline{\phantom{2 \text{ hundreds} + 1 \text{ ten} + 8} \times 4}$

  8 hundreds + 4 tens + 32 ones

= 8 hundreds + 4 tens + (3 tens + 2 ones)

= 8 hundreds + 7 tens + 2 ones

= 872

Standard algorithm

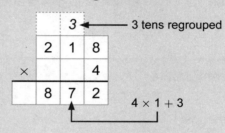

3 tens regrouped

4 × 1 + 3

7. Multiply using the standard algorithm. You may need to regroup more than once.

a) 425 × 3

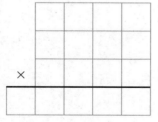

b) 172 × 4

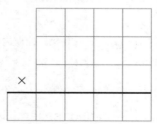

c) 135 × 7

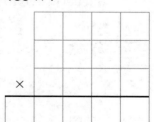

d) 3,145 × 3

e) 6,384 × 9

Bonus ▶ 987,654,321 × 9

8. In football, a touchdown earns 7 points. How many points does a team earn if it scores 43 touchdowns?

A quick way to multiply a whole number by 10, 100, or 1,000 is to write zeros at the end of the whole number.

Examples: $23 \times 10 = 230$ $35 \times 100 = 3,500$ $417 \times 1,000 = 417,000$

9. Multiply mentally.

a) 235×10

$= 2,350$

b) 752×100

c) $48 \times 1,000$

Bonus ▶ $465 \times 10,000$

Multiplication satisfies the **associative property**.

We can use the associative property to multiply 31×200 mentally.

Example: $(2 \times 3) \times 4 = 2 \times (3 \times 4)$

Example: $31 \times 200 = 31 \times (2 \times 100)$
$= (31 \times 2) \times 100$
$= (62 \times 100)$
$= 6,200$

---

10. Multiply mentally.

a) 213×30

$= 6,390$

b) 413×200

c) 121×40

Bonus ▶ $423 \times 20,000$

Multiplication satisfies the **distributive property** over addition or subtraction.

Example: $2 \times (3 + 4) = (2 \times 3) + (2 \times 4)$

---

11. Rewrite using the distributive property.

a) $25 \times (10 + 4)$

$= (25 \times \underline{\ 10\ })$
$+ (25 \times \underline{\ 4\ })$

b) $32 \times (20 + 7)$

$= (32 \times \underline{\quad})$
$+ (32 \times \underline{\quad})$

c) $53 \times (40 + 2)$

$= (53 \times \underline{\quad})$
$+ (53 \times \underline{\quad})$

12. Rewrite the second number, then calculate using the distributive property.

a) 43×21

$= 43 \times (20 + \underline{\ 1\ })$
$= (43 \times 20) + (43 \times \underline{\ 1\ })$
$= 860 + 43$
$= 903$

b) 51×32

$= 51 \times (30 + \underline{\quad})$
$= (51 \times 30) + (51 \times \underline{\quad})$
$=$
$=$
$=$

c) 72×43

$= \underline{\quad} \times (40 + \underline{\quad})$
$=$
$=$
$=$

d) 70×32

$= 70 \times (30 + 2)$

e) 80×47

$= 80 \times (40 + 7)$

f) 90×62

$= 90 \times (60 + 2)$

You can multiply by a 2-digit number in two grids using the distributive property.

56×27

$= 56 \times (20 + 7)$

$= (56 \times 20) + (56 \times 7)$

$= 1,120 + 392$

$= 1,512$

		4		
			5	6
			2	7
×				
		3	9	2
+	1	1	2	0
	1	5	1	2

		1		
			5	6
			2	0
×				
	1	1	2	0

13. Multiply using two grids.

a) 48×32

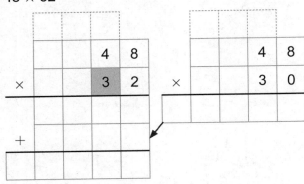

b) 123×58

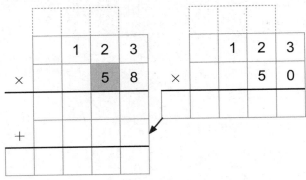

You can multiply by a 2-digit number using one grid to save space.

This is the standard algorithm for multiplying a 2-digit number.

		1		
		4		
			5	6
			2	7
×				
		3	9	2
+	1	1	2	0
	1	5	1	2

$\leftarrow$ 56 × 7

$\leftarrow$ 56 × 20

$\leftarrow$ (56 × 20) + (56 × 7)

14. Multiply using the standard algorithm.

a) 38×42

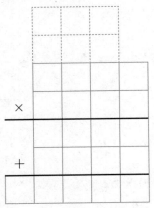

b) 43×79

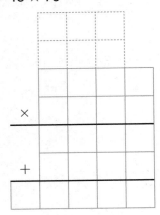

c) 314×26

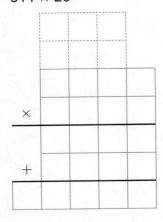

2. Division Review

The division equation $8 \div 2 = 4$ represents two ways of dividing 8 items into equal groups.

                                    or   (○ ○ ○ ○)
                                                                              (○ ○ ○ ○)

8 items with 4 groups of 2 each   8 items with 2 groups of 4 each

1. Write two division equations for the situation.

   a) 15 apples are divided into 5 groups of 3 each. $15 \div 3 = 5$ $15 \div 5 = 3$

   b) 24 pictures are placed on 4 pages.
      Each page has 6 pictures.   _____   _____

   c) $35 is shared among 7 friends.
      Each friend gets $5.   _____   _____

If we divide 23 items into 4 groups, 3 items are left over.

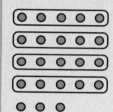

Using **long division** helps you to write a **division equation**.

$$
\begin{array}{r}
5 \leftarrow \text{quotient} \\
\text{divisor} \longrightarrow 4\overline{)23} \leftarrow \text{dividend} \\
-20 \\
\hline
3 \leftarrow \text{remainder}
\end{array}
$$

$23 \div 4 = 5 \text{ R } 3$

---

2. Write a division equation for the long division.

   a)
   $$
   \begin{array}{r}
   5 \\
   7\overline{)38} \\
   -35 \\
   \hline
   3
   \end{array}
   $$

   b)
   $$
   \begin{array}{r}
   7 \\
   4\overline{)30} \\
   -28 \\
   \hline
   2
   \end{array}
   $$

   c)
   $$
   \begin{array}{r}
   9 \\
   6\overline{)58} \\
   -54 \\
   \hline
   4
   \end{array}
   $$

   _____   _____   _____

To do long division:

Step 1: Try a digit for the quotient.

Step 2: Multiply the quotient by the divisor. If the answer is greater than the dividend, try a new quotient.

Step 3: Subtract. The remainder must be less than the divisor.

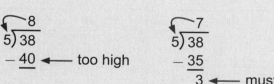

$$
\begin{array}{r}
8 \\
5\overline{)38} \\
-40 \leftarrow \text{too high} \\
\end{array}
\qquad
\begin{array}{r}
7 \\
5\overline{)38} \\
-35 \\
\hline
3 \leftarrow \text{must be less than divisor}
\end{array}
$$

---

3. Divide using long division on grid paper.

   a) $58 \div 7$ b) $76 \div 9$ c) $46 \div 8$

To divide 235 ÷ 5, you will need to regroup:

Step 1: Circle the first group of digits larger than the divisor. 23 is greater than 5, so circle 23 tens in ②③5.

Step 2: Divide the 23 tens into 5 groups.

```
      4   ← 4 tens in each group
  5)②③5   ← 23 tens to be divided into
   - 20       5 groups
   ───
      3   ← 3 tens left over
```

Step 3: The leftover is 3 tens and 5 ones = 35 ones.

```
      47  ← 7 ones in each group
  5)235
   - 20
   ───↓
      ㉟  ← 3 tens + 5 ones = 35 ones
    - 35
    ───
       0
```

4. Divide using long division, then write the division equation.

a) 426 ÷ 6

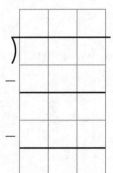

b) 356 ÷ 8

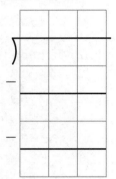

c) 289 ÷ 4

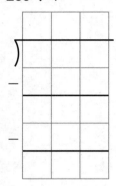

d) 1,371 ÷ 3

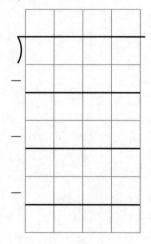

e) 3,120 ÷ 5

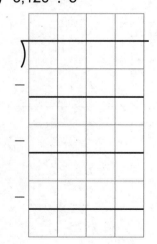

f) 1,602 ÷ 9

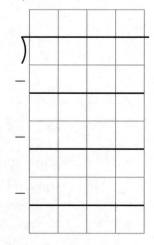

5. Find the number of weeks in 1,095 days.

3. Fractions Review

A fraction names part of a whole. The pie is cut into 8 equal parts. 5 parts out of the 8 are shaded.

So $\frac{5}{8}$ of the pie is shaded.

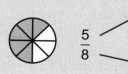

The **numerator** tells you how many parts are shaded.

The **denominator** tells you how many equal parts are in a whole.

1. Write a fraction for the shaded region.

a)

b)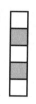

c)

d)

_____   _____   _____   _____

Equivalent fractions show the same part of the same whole.

You can find equivalent fractions by cutting every part of the whole into equal parts.

$\frac{3}{4}$ $\begin{array}{c}\times 2 \\ \times 2\end{array}$ $= \frac{6}{8}$

2. Draw lines to cut the pie into more pieces. Count the number of shaded parts and the number of parts in the whole to find the equivalent fractions.

a)   6 pieces

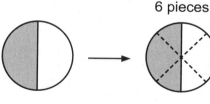

$\frac{1}{2}$ $=$ $\frac{3}{6}$

b)   8 pieces

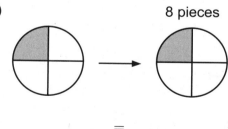

$=$

c)   9 pieces

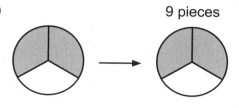

$=$

d)   10 pieces

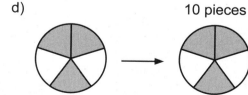

$=$

3. Use multiplication to find an equivalent fraction.

a) $\dfrac{3 \times 5}{4 \times 5} = \dfrac{15}{20}$

b) $\dfrac{5 \times 2}{6 \times 2} =$

c) $\dfrac{4 \times 6}{5 \times 6} =$

d) $\dfrac{5 \times 3}{8 \times 3} =$

4. What number do you multiply the fraction by to get the equivalent fraction?

a) $\dfrac{5 \times 3}{8 \times 3} = \dfrac{15}{24}$

b) $\dfrac{3 \times}{7 \times} = \dfrac{12}{28}$

c) $\dfrac{4 \times}{9 \times} = \dfrac{20}{45}$

d) $\dfrac{1 \times}{6 \times} = \dfrac{7}{42}$

4, 8, ⑫, 16, 20, 24, and so on, are multiples of 4.

6, ⑫, 18, 24, 30, and so on, are multiples of 6.

The **lowest common multiple** (**LCM**) of 4 and 6 is the first number to appear in both lists.

The LCM for 4 and 6 is 12.

---

5. Find the LCM of the numbers.

a) 6, 8   _6, 12, 18, ㉔, 30, 36, …_

   _8, 16, ㉔, 32, 40, 48, …_

   LCM = _24_

b) 10, 15 _____

   _____

   LCM = _____

c) 9, 12 _____

   _____

   LCM = _____

d) 2, 10 _____

   _____

   LCM = _____

e) 4, 10

f) 14, 21

To compare fractions with the same denominator, look at the number of shaded parts for each fraction.

So $\dfrac{5}{8} > \dfrac{3}{8}$ because 5 > 3.

5 shaded parts

3 shaded parts

---

6. Circle the larger fraction.

a) $\dfrac{1}{4}$ and $\dfrac{3}{4}$

b) $\dfrac{7}{8}$ and $\dfrac{5}{8}$

c) $\dfrac{9}{16}$ and $\dfrac{11}{16}$

d) $\dfrac{31}{50}$ and $\dfrac{11}{50}$

7. Circle the smaller fraction.

a) $\dfrac{1}{6}$ and $\dfrac{5}{6}$

b) $\dfrac{3}{5}$ and $\dfrac{2}{5}$

c) $\dfrac{7}{10}$ and $\dfrac{3}{10}$

d) $\dfrac{5}{25}$ and $\dfrac{7}{25}$

To compare fractions with different denominators, you need to find the equivalent fractions.

Example: $\dfrac{5}{6}$, $\dfrac{3}{4}$

Step 1: Find the LCM of the denominators. This is called the **lowest common denominator** (**LCD**).

The LCM of 4 and 6 is 12. So the LCD is 12.

Step 2: Change each fraction to an equivalent fraction with the new denominator.

$\dfrac{5 \times 2}{6 \times 2}$ $\qquad$ $\dfrac{3 \times 3}{4 \times 3}$

$= \dfrac{10}{12}$ $\qquad$ $= \dfrac{9}{12}$

Step 3: Compare the equivalent fractions.

Since $\dfrac{10}{12} > \dfrac{9}{12}$, then $\dfrac{5}{6} > \dfrac{3}{4}$

8. Find the larger fraction by comparing the equivalent fractions.

a) $\dfrac{7}{10}$ and $\dfrac{5}{8}$

b) $\dfrac{7}{9}$ and $\dfrac{11}{12}$

c) $\dfrac{7}{10}$ and $\dfrac{5}{6}$

d) $\dfrac{3}{5}$ and $\dfrac{4}{7}$

LCD = __40__ $\qquad$ LCD = _____ $\qquad$ LCD = _____ $\qquad$ LCD = _____

$\dfrac{7 \times 4}{10 \times 4} = \dfrac{28}{40}$

$\dfrac{5 \times 5}{8 \times 5} = \dfrac{25}{40}$

So $\dfrac{7}{10} > \dfrac{5}{8}$

To add (or subtract) fractions with the same denominator, keep the denominator and add (or subtract) the numerators.

Example:

$\dfrac{3}{7}$ of the squares are shaded dark.

$\dfrac{2}{7}$ of the squares are shaded light.

So $\dfrac{3}{7} + \dfrac{2}{7} = \dfrac{5}{7}$ of the squares are shaded.

9. Add or subtract.

a) $\dfrac{3}{8} + \dfrac{4}{8} =$

b) $\dfrac{9}{10} - \dfrac{2}{10} =$

c) $\dfrac{3}{16} + \dfrac{8}{16} =$

d) $\dfrac{18}{30} - \dfrac{5}{30} =$

e) $\dfrac{3}{7} - \dfrac{1}{7} + \dfrac{4}{7} =$

f) $\dfrac{3}{8} + \dfrac{3}{8} - \dfrac{1}{8} =$

g) $\dfrac{4}{9} + \dfrac{4}{9} - \dfrac{3}{9} =$

h) $\dfrac{13}{15} - \dfrac{4}{15} - \dfrac{2}{15} =$

To add or subtract fractions with different denominators:

Example: $\dfrac{3}{8} + \dfrac{1}{6}$

Step 1: Find the lowest common denominator.

$8 \longrightarrow 8, 16, 24, 32, 40, \ldots$
$6 \longrightarrow 12, 18, 24, 30, 36, \ldots$
LCD = 24

Step 2: Find the equivalent fractions using the LCD as the denominator.

$\dfrac{3 \times 3}{8 \times 3} = \dfrac{9}{24}$ $\dfrac{1 \times 4}{6 \times 4} = \dfrac{4}{24}$

Step 3: Add or subtract the equivalent fractions.

$\dfrac{9}{24} + \dfrac{4}{24} = \dfrac{13}{24}$

10. Add or subtract.

a) $\dfrac{7}{9} - \dfrac{5}{12}$ LCD = ___36___

$= \dfrac{7 \times 4}{9 \times 4} - \dfrac{5 \times 3}{12 \times 3}$

$= \dfrac{28}{36} - \dfrac{15}{36}$

$= \dfrac{13}{36}$

b) $\dfrac{5}{6} + \dfrac{3}{10}$ LCD = _____

c) $\dfrac{7}{12} - \dfrac{3}{8}$ LCD = _____

d) $\dfrac{3}{8} + \dfrac{1}{5}$

e) $\dfrac{3}{4} - \dfrac{1}{2}$

f) $\dfrac{7}{10} - \dfrac{2}{15}$

You can also think of a fraction as division.

Example: $\dfrac{8}{4}$ 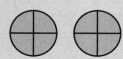   8 parts shaded
4 parts in the whole

There are $8 \div 4 = 2$ whole pies.

11. Write the fraction as a division.

a) $\dfrac{8}{4} = 8 \div 4$

b) $\dfrac{15}{5} =$

c) $\dfrac{3}{4} =$

d) $\dfrac{9}{10} =$

12. Write the division as a fraction.

a) $18 \div 6 = \dfrac{18}{6}$

b) $20 \div 4 =$

c) $7 \div 8 =$

d) $11 \div 16 =$

4. Reducing Fractions

Reduced fractions are equivalent fractions with fewer parts in the whole.

You can reduce fractions by combining equal parts of the whole to make fewer parts.

$$\frac{6}{8} = \frac{6 \div 2}{8 \div 2} = \frac{3}{4}$$

1. Use division to find a reduced fraction.

a) $\dfrac{15 \div 5}{20 \div 5} = \dfrac{3}{4}$　　　　b) $\dfrac{15 \div 3}{24 \div 3} =$　　　　c) $\dfrac{18 \div 2}{20 \div 2} =$　　　　d) $\dfrac{30 \div 6}{42 \div 6} =$

The factors of 12 are 1, 2, 3, 4, ⑥, and 12.

The factors of 18 are 1, 2, 3, ⑥, 9, and 18.

The **greatest common factor** (**GCF**) is the greatest number that appears in both lists.

The GCF of 12 and 18 is 6.

---

2. Find the GCF of the numbers.

a) 10, 15 　 _1, 2, ⑤, 10_

　　　　　　 _1, 3, ⑤, 15_

　　　　　 GCF = _5_

b) 8, 12 　_____

　　　　　_____

　　　　 GCF = _____

c) 24, 32 　_____

　　　　　_____

　　　　 GCF = _____

d) 27, 36 　_____

　　　　　_____

　　　　 GCF = _____

A fraction is in **lowest terms** if the GCF of the numerator and denominator is 1.

$\dfrac{3}{4}$ is in lowest terms because the GCF of 3 and 4 is 1.

$\dfrac{6}{9}$ is not in lowest terms because the GCF of 6 and 9 is 3.

---

3. Write the GCF of the numerator and denominator. Circle the fraction if it is in lowest terms.

a) $\dfrac{9}{12}$　　b) ⟨$\dfrac{5}{7}$⟩　　c) $\dfrac{10}{15}$　　d) $\dfrac{3}{8}$　　e) $\dfrac{9}{14}$　　f) $\dfrac{14}{28}$

　 GCF = _3_　　GCF = _1_　　GCF = _____　　GCF = _____　　GCF = _____　　GCF = _____

To reduce a fraction to lowest terms, divide the numerator and denominator by the GCF.

Example: $\dfrac{12}{15}$

Step 1: Find the GCF of the numerator and denominator.

$12 \longrightarrow 1, 2, ③, 4, 6, 12$
$15 \longrightarrow 1, ③, 5, 15$

$GCF = 3$

Step 2: Divide both the numerator and the denominator by the GCF.

$\dfrac{12 \div 3}{15 \div 3} = \dfrac{4}{5}$

4. Reduce the fraction to lowest terms.

a) $\dfrac{10}{12}$ GCF = __2__

$= \dfrac{10 \div 2}{12 \div 2}$

$= \dfrac{5}{6}$

b) $\dfrac{15}{20}$ GCF = _____

c) $\dfrac{18}{24}$ GCF = _____

d) $\dfrac{12}{27}$ GCF = _____

e) $\dfrac{12}{32}$

f) $\dfrac{14}{21}$

g) $\dfrac{27}{45}$

Bonus ▶ $\dfrac{100}{150}$

5. Add or subtract the fractions. Reduce your answer to lowest terms.

a) $\dfrac{3}{8} + \dfrac{3}{8}$

$= \dfrac{6}{8}$

$= \dfrac{6 \div 2}{8 \div 2}$

$= \dfrac{3}{4}$

b) $\dfrac{7}{12} - \dfrac{1}{12}$

c) $\dfrac{4}{15} + \dfrac{8}{15}$

d) $\dfrac{7}{9} - \dfrac{1}{9}$

6. Add or subtract the fractions. You will need to find the LCD of the fractions. Reduce your answer to lowest terms.

a) $\dfrac{1}{3} + \dfrac{1}{6}$

b) $\dfrac{9}{10} - \dfrac{11}{15}$

c) $\dfrac{1}{6} + \dfrac{1}{12}$

Bonus ▶ $\dfrac{21}{100} - \dfrac{31}{300}$

7. Zack thinks that a fraction is in lowest terms if he cannot reduce it any further. Is he correct? Explain using the GCF.

5. Multiplying Fractions

Here is $\frac{1}{3}$ of a rectangle.

Here is $\frac{1}{2}$ of $\frac{1}{3}$ of a rectangle.

Extend the line to find the fraction that is shaded.

$$\frac{1}{2} \text{ of } \frac{1}{3} = \frac{1}{6}$$

The word "of" can mean multiply. So you can write $\frac{1}{2}$ of $\frac{1}{3} = \frac{1}{6}$ as $\frac{1}{2} \times \frac{1}{3} = \frac{1}{6}$.

1. Extend the horizontal lines. Then complete the multiplication equation.

a)

$$\frac{1}{3} \times \frac{1}{2} = \frac{1}{6}$$

b)

$$\frac{1}{4} \times \frac{1}{2} =$$

c)

$$\frac{1}{4} \times \frac{1}{3} =$$

d)

$$\frac{1}{2} \times \frac{1}{5} =$$

To find the denominator when multiplying unit fractions, multiply the denominators.

Example: $\frac{1}{3} \times \frac{1}{4} = \frac{1}{12}$ ⟵ $3 \times 4 = 12$

---

2. Multiply.

a) $\frac{1}{3} \times \frac{1}{6} =$

b) $\frac{1}{4} \times \frac{1}{5} =$

c) $\frac{1}{7} \times \frac{1}{3} =$

d) $\frac{1}{9} \times \frac{1}{5} =$

Here is $\frac{2}{3}$ of a rectangle.

Here is $\frac{4}{5}$ of $\frac{2}{3}$ of a rectangle.

Extend the line to find the fraction that is shaded.

$$\frac{4}{5} \times \frac{2}{3} = \frac{8}{15}$$

---

3. Extend the horizontal lines. Then complete the multiplication equation.

a)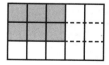

$$\frac{2}{3} \times \frac{3}{5} = \frac{6}{15}$$

b)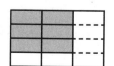

$$\frac{3}{4} \times \frac{2}{3} =$$

c)

$$\frac{2}{5} \times \frac{3}{7} =$$

d)

$$\frac{3}{4} \times \frac{2}{5} =$$

To multiply fractions, multiply the numerators and denominators separately.

Example: $\dfrac{2}{3} \times \dfrac{4}{7} = \dfrac{8}{21}$ ← $2 \times 4 = 8$ ← $3 \times 7 = 21$

4. Multiply.

a) $\dfrac{3}{4} \times \dfrac{5}{8} =$

b) $\dfrac{4}{7} \times \dfrac{2}{9} =$

c) $\dfrac{2}{5} \times \dfrac{4}{7} =$

d) $\dfrac{2}{3} \times \dfrac{7}{9} =$

5. Multiply. Reduce your answer to lowest terms.

a) $\dfrac{3}{4} \times \dfrac{5}{6}$

$= \dfrac{15}{24}$

$= \dfrac{5}{8}$

b) $\dfrac{3}{5} \times \dfrac{4}{9}$

c) $\dfrac{5}{6} \times \dfrac{4}{7}$

d) $\dfrac{5}{9} \times \dfrac{6}{10}$

$\dfrac{9}{4}$ is an **improper fraction** because the numerator is greater than the denominator.

You can multiply improper fractions the same way you multiply proper fractions. Example:

$\dfrac{7}{5} =$

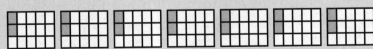

$\dfrac{2}{3} \times \dfrac{7}{5} =$ $= \dfrac{14}{15}$ ← 7 groups of 2 are shaded ← 5 groups of 3 in each whole

6. Multiply. Reduce your answer to lowest terms.

a) $\dfrac{3}{4} \times \dfrac{5}{3}$

$= \dfrac{15}{12}$

$= \dfrac{5}{4}$

b) $\dfrac{2}{3} \times \dfrac{9}{4}$

c) $\dfrac{3}{4} \times \dfrac{8}{7}$

d) $\dfrac{9}{4} \times \dfrac{8}{3}$

7. Claire was given $\dfrac{3}{4}$ of her weekly allowance on Monday. On Tuesday, she spent $\dfrac{2}{3}$ of the money she received on Monday.

a) What fraction of her allowance did she spend on Tuesday?

b) What fraction of her allowance is left?

You can simplify the multiplication.

Example: $\dfrac{5}{6} \times \dfrac{8}{7} = \dfrac{5 \times \circled{8}}{7 \times \circled{6}}$ ← commutative property

Step 1: Find the GCF of one number from the numerators and one number from the denominators.

The GCF of 8 and 6 is 2.

Step 2: Divide one number from the numerators and one number from the denominators by the GCF.

You can divide without switching the order.

$\dfrac{5}{6 \div 2} \times \dfrac{8 \div 2}{7} = \dfrac{5}{3} \times \dfrac{4}{7}$

8. Simplify the multiplication using the steps above.

a) $\dfrac{\circled{9}}{7} \times \dfrac{5}{\circled{12}}$ GCF = 3

$= \dfrac{9 \div 3}{7} \times \dfrac{5}{12 \div 3}$

$= \dfrac{3}{7} \times \dfrac{5}{4}$

b) $\dfrac{\circled{10}}{\circled{15}} \times \dfrac{7}{8}$ GCF = 5

$= \dfrac{10 \div 5}{15 \div 5} \times \dfrac{7}{8}$

c) $\dfrac{8}{\circled{9}} \times \dfrac{\circled{6}}{5}$ GCF = 3

d) $\dfrac{10}{12} \times \dfrac{5}{3}$ GCF = 2

e) $\dfrac{16}{9} \times \dfrac{7}{20}$ GCF = 4

f) $\dfrac{12}{7} \times \dfrac{5}{18}$ GCF = 6

9. Simplify the multiplication as much as possible, then multiply.

a) $\dfrac{5}{\circled{12}} \times \dfrac{\circled{8}}{3}$

$= \dfrac{5}{12 \div 4} \times \dfrac{8 \div 4}{3}$

$= \dfrac{5}{3} \times \dfrac{2}{3}$

$= \dfrac{10}{9}$

b) $\dfrac{15}{10} \times \dfrac{7}{11}$

c) $\dfrac{8}{12} \times \dfrac{9}{5}$

d) $\dfrac{14}{5} \times \dfrac{3}{21}$

e) $\dfrac{20}{7} \times \dfrac{4}{30}$

f) $\dfrac{15}{9} \times \dfrac{10}{14}$

6. Dividing Fractions

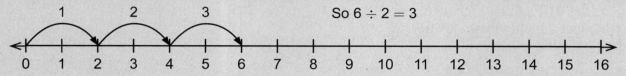

To divide 6 ÷ 2 using a number line, find the number of steps it takes to get to 6 when counting by 2s.

So 6 ÷ 2 = 3

1. Use the number line above to divide.

   a) 12 ÷ 3 =   b) 16 ÷ 8 =   c) 12 ÷ 2 =   d) 15 ÷ 3 =

2. Label the missing fractions on the number line.

   a)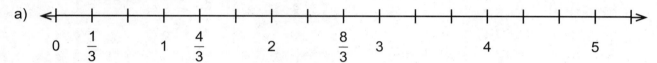

   b)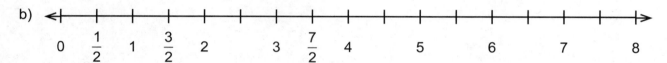

   c)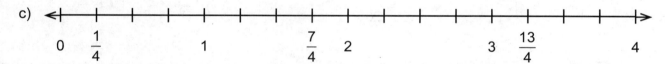

   d)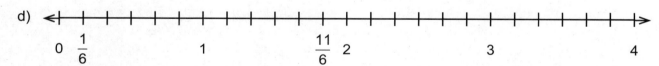

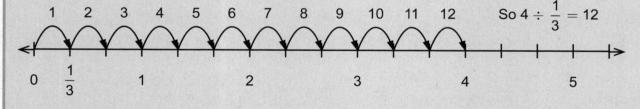

To divide $4 \div \frac{1}{3}$ using a number line, find the number of steps it takes to get to 4 when counting by $\frac{1}{3}$.

So $4 \div \frac{1}{3} = 12$

3. Use a number line from Question 2 to divide by the unit fraction.

   a) $5 \div \frac{1}{2} =$ b) $3 \div \frac{1}{4} =$ c) $5 \div \frac{1}{3} =$ d) $3 \div \frac{1}{6} =$

   e) $5 \div \frac{1}{3} =$ f) $7 \div \frac{1}{2} =$ g) $2 \div \frac{1}{6} =$ h) $4 \div \frac{1}{4} =$

There are 3 thirds in one whole. There are $4 \times 3 = 12$ thirds in 4 wholes.

1			2			3			4		
$\frac{1}{3}$	$\frac{1}{3}$	$\frac{1}{3}$	$\frac{1}{3}$	$\frac{1}{3}$	$\frac{1}{3}$	$\frac{1}{3}$	$\frac{1}{3}$	$\frac{1}{3}$	$\frac{1}{3}$	$\frac{1}{3}$	$\frac{1}{3}$

$$3 \quad + \quad 3 \quad + \quad 3 \quad + \quad 3 \quad = \quad 12 \qquad \text{So } 4 \div \frac{1}{3} = 12$$

4. Use multiplication to divide by a fraction.

a) $4 \div \dfrac{1}{3}$ 　　　　b) $2 \div \dfrac{1}{3}$ 　　　　c) $5 \div \dfrac{1}{4}$ 　　　　d) $3 \div \dfrac{1}{6}$

$= 4 \times 3$

$= 12$

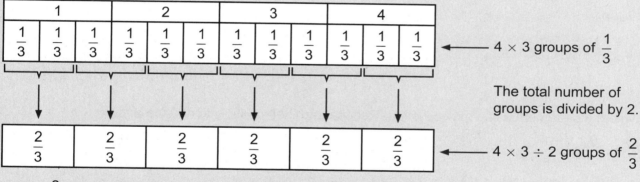

To divide $4 \div \dfrac{2}{3}$, count the number of $\dfrac{2}{3}$ in 4. You can use $4 \div \dfrac{1}{3}$ to help.

4×3 groups of $\dfrac{1}{3}$

The total number of groups is divided by 2.

$4 \times 3 \div 2$ groups of $\dfrac{2}{3}$

So $4 \div \dfrac{2}{3} = 4 \times 3 \div 2 = 6$

5. Calculate using multiplication and division.

a) $6 \div \dfrac{3}{4}$ 　　　　b) $9 \div \dfrac{3}{5}$ 　　　　c) $12 \div \dfrac{3}{8}$ 　　　　d) $10 \div \dfrac{5}{6}$

$= 6 \times 4 \div 3$

$= 8$

e) $6 \div \dfrac{2}{3}$ 　　　　f) $10 \div \dfrac{2}{5}$ 　　　　g) $16 \div \dfrac{2}{3}$ 　　　　h) $15 \div \dfrac{5}{8}$

REMINDER: You can write $5 \div 4$ as the fraction $\dfrac{5}{4}$.

6. Rewrite the statement using multiplication by a fraction.

a) $6 \div \dfrac{3}{4}$

$= 6 \times 4 \div 3$

$= 6 \times \dfrac{4}{3}$

b) $8 \div \dfrac{4}{5}$

c) $14 \div \dfrac{7}{8}$

d) $12 \div \dfrac{4}{7}$

To find the **reciprocal** of a fraction, switch the numerator and the denominator.

Example: The reciprocal of $\dfrac{3}{4}$ is $\dfrac{4}{3}$.

7. Rewrite the statement using multiplication by the reciprocal of the second number.

a) $10 \div \dfrac{5}{3}$

$= 10 \times \dfrac{3}{5}$

b) $12 \div \dfrac{6}{5}$

c) $32 \div \dfrac{8}{3}$

d) $28 \div \dfrac{7}{4}$

8. Rewrite the statement using multiplication. Reduce and then multiply to find the answer.

a) $14 \div \dfrac{7}{3}$

$= \dfrac{14 \div 7}{1} \times \dfrac{3}{7 \div 7}$

$= \dfrac{2}{1} \times \dfrac{3}{1}$

$= 6$

b) $20 \div \dfrac{4}{3}$

c) $48 \div \dfrac{6}{7}$

d) $27 \div \dfrac{9}{4}$

9. Divide using multiplication by the reciprocal.

a) $\dfrac{4}{5} \div \dfrac{8}{3}$

b) $\dfrac{10}{3} \div \dfrac{15}{7}$

c) $\dfrac{12}{5} \div \dfrac{9}{4}$

d) $\dfrac{15}{14} \div \dfrac{10}{21}$

10. In construction, a piece of wood that is called a two-by-four is actually less than 4 inches wide. Nina is building a deck using two-by-fours that are $\dfrac{7}{2}$ inches wide. How many two-by-fours will she need to place side by side to make a floor $\dfrac{254}{4}$ inches wide?

7. Mixed Numbers and Improper Fractions

A **mixed number** is made up of a whole number and a proper fraction.

The total number of quarter pieces is $2 \times 4 + 3 = 11$.

$\dfrac{11}{4}$ is an **improper fraction** because the numerator is greater than the denominator.

Example: $2\dfrac{3}{4}$

$2\dfrac{3}{4} = \dfrac{11}{4}$

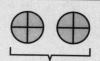

2 whole pies $\dfrac{3}{4}$ of a pie

1. Write the mixed number as an improper fraction.

   a) $3\dfrac{1}{4} =$

   b) $2\dfrac{3}{8} =$

   c) $4\dfrac{5}{6} =$

   d) $5\dfrac{1}{2} =$

To change $\dfrac{11}{4}$ into a mixed number, divide the numerator by the denominator.

$11 \div 4 = 2\ R\ 3$

$\dfrac{11}{4} = 2\dfrac{3}{4}$

2. Write the improper fraction as a mixed number.

   a) $\dfrac{7}{3} =$

   b) $\dfrac{29}{6} =$

   c) $\dfrac{35}{8} =$

   d) $\dfrac{47}{10} =$

Sometimes you need to regroup the fractional part. To regroup, change the improper fraction to a mixed number and then add the whole parts.

Example:

$5\dfrac{7}{4} = 5 + 1\dfrac{3}{4} = 6\dfrac{3}{4}$

3. Write the mixed number as a mixed number with a proper fraction.

   a) $1\dfrac{5}{3}$

   b) $2\dfrac{11}{8}$

   c) $4\dfrac{11}{6}$

   d) $12\dfrac{9}{5}$

To add mixed numbers, add the whole numbers and fractions separately. Write the answer as a mixed number with a whole number and a proper fraction.

Example:

$2\dfrac{3}{7} + 8\dfrac{6}{7} = 10\dfrac{9}{7} = 10 + 1\dfrac{2}{7} = 11\dfrac{2}{7}$

4. Add. Write your answer as a whole number and a proper fraction.

   a) $1\dfrac{3}{5} + 8\dfrac{4}{5}$

   b) $3\dfrac{5}{8} + 2\dfrac{6}{8}$

   c) $4\dfrac{5}{7} + 2\dfrac{6}{7}$

   d) $6\dfrac{5}{9} + 4\dfrac{8}{9}$

5. Add. You will need to find the LCD (lowest common denominator) of the fractions. Write the answer as a mixed number with a proper fraction.

a) $1\frac{2}{3} + 2\frac{3}{4}$

$= 1\frac{8}{12} + 2\frac{9}{12}$

$= 3\frac{17}{12}$

$= 4\frac{5}{12}$

b) $4\frac{5}{6} + 1\frac{3}{8}$

c) $3\frac{7}{14} + 2\frac{5}{21}$

You can subtract mixed numbers by subtracting the whole numbers and the fractions separately.

Example:

$$6\frac{5}{7} - 2\frac{4}{7} = (6-2) + \left(\frac{5}{7} - \frac{4}{7}\right) = 4 + \frac{1}{7} = 4\frac{1}{7}$$

---

6. Subtract. Write your answer as a whole number and a proper fraction.

a) $8\frac{3}{5} - 4\frac{2}{5} = 4\frac{1}{5}$

b) $9\frac{5}{8} - 2\frac{4}{8} =$

c) $7\frac{7}{9} - 6\frac{5}{9} =$

To subtract $6\frac{2}{7} - 3\frac{4}{7}$, you need to regroup because we can't subtract $\frac{4}{7}$ from $\frac{2}{7}$.

Step 1: Regroup the first mixed number.

Subtract 1 from 6 and add to $\frac{2}{7}$

$$6\frac{2}{7} = 5 + 1\frac{2}{7} = 5 + \frac{9}{7} = 5\frac{9}{7}$$

Step 2: Subtract the whole numbers and fractions separately.

$$6\frac{2}{7} - 3\frac{4}{7} = 5\frac{9}{7} - 3\frac{4}{7} = 2\frac{5}{7}$$

---

7. Subtract by regrouping the first mixed number.

a) $4\frac{3}{8} - 2\frac{6}{8}$

$= 3\frac{11}{8} - 2\frac{6}{8}$

$= 1\frac{5}{8}$

b) $7\frac{1}{5} - 3\frac{3}{5}$

c) $4\frac{1}{6} - 1\frac{5}{6}$

d) $5\frac{1}{4} - 2\frac{3}{4}$

e) $2\frac{5}{8} - 1\frac{7}{8}$

f) $1\frac{1}{3} - \frac{2}{3}$

8. Subtract. You will need to find the LCD of the fractions. You might also have to regroup.

a) $7\dfrac{5}{6} - 2\dfrac{1}{8}$

b) $5\dfrac{1}{4} - 2\dfrac{5}{6}$

c) $9\dfrac{3}{10} - 3\dfrac{7}{15}$

d) $10\dfrac{1}{8} - 2\dfrac{5}{12}$

9. Add or subtract. Write your answer as a mixed number in lowest terms.

a) $6\dfrac{1}{2} - 2\dfrac{5}{6}$

b) $2\dfrac{1}{10} + 4\dfrac{3}{15}$

c) $5\dfrac{1}{8} - 2\dfrac{3}{4}$

d) $2\dfrac{4}{9} + 6\dfrac{5}{12}$

$= 6\dfrac{3}{6} - 2\dfrac{5}{6}$

$= 5\dfrac{9}{6} - 2\dfrac{5}{6}$

$= 3\dfrac{4}{6}$

$= 3\dfrac{2}{3}$

To multiply mixed fractions:

Example: $1\dfrac{3}{4} \times 2\dfrac{2}{3}$

Step 1: Change to improper fractions.

$= \dfrac{7}{4} \times \dfrac{8}{3}$

Step 2: Reduce, and then multiply.

$= \dfrac{7}{4 \div 4} \times \dfrac{8 \div 4}{3} = \dfrac{7}{1} \times \dfrac{2}{3} = \dfrac{14}{3} = 4\dfrac{2}{3}$

---

10. Multiply. Write your answer as a mixed number in lowest terms.

a) $4\dfrac{1}{2} \times 1\dfrac{4}{9}$

b) $2\dfrac{4}{5} \times 3\dfrac{3}{4}$

c) $2\dfrac{1}{2} \times 2\dfrac{1}{5}$

d) $3\dfrac{6}{7} \times 2\dfrac{1}{3}$

To divide mixed fractions:

Example: $2\dfrac{1}{8} \div 1\dfrac{3}{4}$

Step 1: Change to improper fractions.

$= \dfrac{17}{8} \div \dfrac{7}{4}$

Step 2: Multiply by the reciprocal of the second fraction. Reduce, and then multiply.

$= \dfrac{17}{8 \div 4} \times \dfrac{4 \div 4}{7} = \dfrac{17}{2} \times \dfrac{1}{7} = \dfrac{17}{14} = 1\dfrac{3}{14}$

---

11. Divide. Write your answer as a mixed number in lowest terms.

a) $2\dfrac{5}{8} \div 2\dfrac{1}{3}$

b) $3\dfrac{3}{7} \div 2\dfrac{4}{5}$

c) $4\dfrac{4}{9} \div 2\dfrac{6}{7}$

d) $4\dfrac{7}{10} \div 2\dfrac{4}{5}$

8. Order of Operations

Mathematicians use a standard order of operations.

1. Do operations in brackets.

2. Do all multiplications and divisions, from left to right.

3. Do all additions and subtractions, from left to right.

1. Circle the operation you would do first.

a) $6 + \boxed{5 \times 2}$

b) $5 \times (8 - 4)$

c) $8 \times 7 - 3$

d) $4 \times 8 \div 3$

e) $9 - 3 + 6$

f) $(6 - 4) \times 9$

g) $12 - 3 - 8$

h) $36 \div 6 \div 3$

i) $42 \div (6 \div 2)$

2. Do the operations one at a time, in the standard order.

a) $6 + 5 \times (7 - 3)$

$= 6 + 5 \times 4$

$= 6 + 20$

$= 26$

b) $24 \div 3 + 7 \times 5$

c) $12 - 15 \div (7 - 2)$

d) $7 \times 2 \div (8 - 6)$

e) $24 - 12 \div (7 - 4)$

f) $(15 + 13) \div (1 + 2 \times 3)$

3. Find the value of the expression using the standard order of operations.

a) $8 + \dfrac{15}{5}$

$= 8 + 15 \div 5$

$= 8 + 3$

$= 11$

b) $12 - \dfrac{24}{6} + 5$

c) $\dfrac{28}{4} + 6 - \dfrac{35}{5}$

d) $\dfrac{42}{6} - \dfrac{10}{2}$

e) $5 \times \left(3 + \dfrac{8}{2}\right)$

f) $(5 + 4) \times \dfrac{10}{2}$

The expression $\dfrac{8+5\times4}{6-2}$ means $\dfrac{(8+5\times4)}{(6-2)}$. Calculate the numerator and denominator separately.

4. Write brackets around the numerator and denominator, then calculate.

a) $\dfrac{3+4\times6}{11-2}$

b) $\dfrac{27-15\div5}{2+3\times2}$

c) $\dfrac{15+12\div4}{10-2\times4}$

$= \dfrac{(3+4\times6)}{(11-2)}$

$= \dfrac{(3+24)}{9}$

$= \dfrac{27}{9}$

$= 3$

Calculations with fractions follow the same order of operations.

5. Calculate using the standard order of operations. Reduce your answer to lowest terms.

a) $\dfrac{2}{3}+\dfrac{5}{8}\times\dfrac{4}{3}$

b) $\left(\dfrac{3}{4}+\dfrac{1}{2}\right)\times\dfrac{6}{7}$

c) $\dfrac{3}{2}-\dfrac{1}{6}\div\dfrac{2}{9}$

$= \dfrac{2}{3}+\dfrac{5}{8\div4}\times\dfrac{4\div4}{3}$

$= \dfrac{2}{3}+\dfrac{5}{2}\times\dfrac{1}{3}$

$= \dfrac{2}{3}+\dfrac{5}{6}$

$= \dfrac{4}{6}+\dfrac{5}{6}$

$= \dfrac{9}{6}$

$= \dfrac{3}{2}$

d) $\left(\dfrac{3}{4}-\dfrac{1}{6}\right)\times\dfrac{6}{5}$

e) $\left(\dfrac{1}{3}\div\dfrac{1}{4}\right)\div\dfrac{1}{6}$

f) $\dfrac{1}{3}\div\left(\dfrac{1}{4}\div\dfrac{1}{6}\right)$

g) $\left(\dfrac{1}{2}+\dfrac{1}{3}\right)\div\dfrac{7}{12}$

h) $\dfrac{2}{3}\div\dfrac{5}{6}+\dfrac{1}{5}$

i) $\left(\dfrac{5}{8}-\dfrac{1}{4}\right)\div\dfrac{5}{8}$

9. Decimal Review

In a **decimal fraction**, the denominator is a power of 10.

10, 100, 1,000, and so on, are powers of 10.

Examples: $\frac{7}{10}$, $\frac{23}{100}$, and $\frac{247}{1,000}$ are decimal fractions.

1. Find the missing equivalent decimal fractions.

a) $\frac{7}{10} = \frac{70}{100}$

b) $\frac{35}{100} = \frac{}{1,000}$

c) $\frac{}{10} = \frac{900}{1,000}$

d) $\frac{3}{10} = \frac{30}{100} = \frac{300}{1,000}$

e) $\frac{}{10} = \frac{90}{100} = \frac{}{1,000}$

f) $\frac{}{10} = \frac{}{100} = \frac{500}{1,000}$

Decimals are a way to record place values based on decimal fractions.

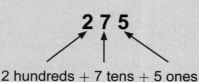

2 7 5

2 hundreds + 7 tens + 5 ones

0.2 7 5 ⟵ decimal point

2 tenths + 7 hundredths + 5 thousandths

$$\frac{2}{10} + \frac{7}{100} + \frac{5}{1,000}$$

2. Write the number in expanded form.

a) $2.35 = \underline{\quad 2 \quad} + \frac{3}{10} + \frac{5}{100}$

b) $3.49 = \underline{\quad\quad} + \frac{}{10} + \frac{}{100}$

c) $4.178 = \underline{\quad\quad} + \frac{}{10} + \frac{}{100} + \frac{}{1,000}$

d) $7.490 = \underline{\quad\quad} + \frac{}{10} + \frac{}{100} + \frac{}{1,000}$

e) $9.073 = \underline{\quad\quad} + \frac{}{10} + \frac{}{100} + \frac{}{1,000}$

f) $6.102 = \underline{\quad\quad} + \frac{}{10} + \frac{}{100} + \frac{}{1,000}$

3. Write the expanded form as a decimal.

a) $2 + \frac{3}{10} + \frac{9}{100} + \frac{1}{1,000} = \underline{\quad 2.391 \quad}$

b) $7 + \frac{2}{10} + \frac{3}{100} + \frac{4}{1,000} = \underline{\quad\quad\quad}$

c) $9 + \frac{3}{10} + \frac{0}{100} + \frac{5}{1,000} = \underline{\quad\quad\quad}$

d) $4 + \frac{0}{10} + \frac{6}{100} + \frac{8}{1,000} = \underline{\quad\quad\quad}$

Bonus ▶

e) $4 + \frac{1}{10} + \frac{6}{1,000} = \underline{\quad\quad\quad}$

f) $2 + \frac{3}{100} + \frac{6}{1,000} = \underline{\quad\quad\quad}$

You can write 0.27 as a single fraction: $0.27 = \dfrac{2}{10} + \dfrac{7}{100} = \dfrac{20}{100} + \dfrac{7}{100} = \dfrac{27}{100}$

You can write 0.135 as a single fraction: $0.135 = \dfrac{1}{10} + \dfrac{3}{100} + \dfrac{5}{1,000} = \dfrac{100}{1,000} + \dfrac{30}{1,000} + \dfrac{5}{1,000} = \dfrac{135}{1,000}$

4. Write the decimal as a single fraction.

a) $0.37 = \dfrac{37}{100}$
　　b) $0.28 = \dfrac{}{100}$
　　c) $0.43 = \dfrac{}{}$
　　d) $0.07 = \dfrac{}{}$

e) $0.219 = \dfrac{219}{1,000}$
　　f) $0.614 = \dfrac{}{1,000}$
　　g) $0.438 = \dfrac{}{}$
　　h) $0.029 = \dfrac{}{}$

Multiplying by 10 moves the decimal point 1 place to the right.
　　$0.37 \times 10 = \dfrac{37}{100} \times 10 = \dfrac{370}{100} = 3 + \dfrac{70}{100} = 3.70$

0	0 .	3	7	0	0

---

5. Multiply by 10 by moving the decimal point.

a) 3.5×10

$= \underline{\;35.0\;}$

b) 0.47×10

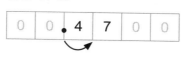

$= \underline{}$

c) 38.0×10

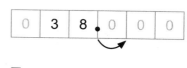

$= \underline{}$

Multiplying by 100 moves the decimal point 2 places to the right.
　　$0.028 \times 100 = \dfrac{28}{1,000} \times 100 = \dfrac{2,800}{1,000} = 2 + \dfrac{800}{1,000} = 2.800$

---

6. Multiply by 100 by moving the decimal point.

a) 2.9×100

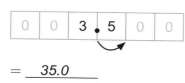

$= \underline{\;290.0\;}$

b) 0.36×100

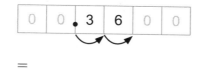

$= \underline{}$

c) 52.4×100

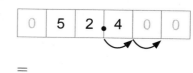

$= \underline{}$

---

7. Multiply.

a) $9.28 \times 10 = \underline{}$
　　b) $0.063 \times 100 = \underline{}$
　　c) $2.367 \times 10 = \underline{}$

d) $0.0045 \times 100 = \underline{}$
　　e) $0.4 \times 10 = \underline{}$
　　f) $6.1 \times 100 = \underline{}$

g) $0.65 \times 10 = \underline{}$
　　h) $0.0043 \times 100 = \underline{}$
　　i) $8.34 \times 100 = \underline{}$

Dividing by 10 moves the decimal point
1 place to the left.

$$0.37 \div 10 = \frac{37}{100} \div 10 = \frac{37}{1,000} = 0.037$$

8. Divide by 10 by moving the decimal point.

a) $2.8 \div 10$

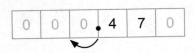

= ___0.28___

b) $0.47 \div 10$

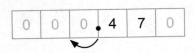

= _____

c) $75 \div 10$

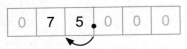

= _____

Dividing by 100 moves the decimal point
2 places to the left.

$$2.7 \div 100 = \frac{27}{10} \div 100 = \frac{27}{1,000} = 0.027$$

9. Divide by 100 by moving the decimal point.

a) $9.6 \div 100$

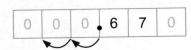

= ___0.096___

b) $0.67 \div 100$

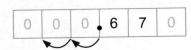

= _____

c) $81.3 \div 100$

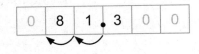

= _____

10. Divide.

a) $5.18 \div 10 =$ _____

b) $0.63 \div 100 =$ _____

c) $2.36 \div 10 =$ _____

d) $0.048 \div 100 =$ _____

e) $0.3 \div 10 =$ _____

f) $7.4 \div 100 =$ _____

11. Use the grid to calculate.

a)	7.635×100	0	0	7.	6	3	5	0	0	763.5
b)	$0.354 \div 10$	0	0	0.	3	5	4	0	0	0.0354
c)	0.89×10	0	0	0	0	0	0	0	0	
d)	$23.76 \div 100$	0	0	0	0	0	0	0	0	
e)	0.0034×100	0	0	0	0	0	0	0	0	
f)	$0.56 \div 100$	0	0	0	0	0	0	0	0	
g)	9.23×100	0	0	0	0	0	0	0	0	
h)	$0.12 \times 1,000$	0	0	0	0	0	0	0	0	
i)	$7.56 \div 1,000$	0	0	0	0	0	0	0	0	

10. Operations With Decimals

Decimals can be written as decimal fractions. The number of decimal digits is the same as the number of zeros in the denominator.

Examples: $0.3 = \dfrac{3}{10}$ $0.37 = \dfrac{37}{100}$ $0.371 = \dfrac{371}{1,000}$

1. Write as a decimal fraction.

a) 0.35 =

b) 0.7 =

c) 0.275 =

d) 0.0249 =

We can add or subtract decimals as decimal fractions. $0.27 + 0.34 = \dfrac{27}{100} + \dfrac{34}{100} = \dfrac{61}{100} = 0.61$

2. Add or subtract as decimal fractions.

a) 0.5 + 0.3

b) 0.48 − 0.23

c) 0.416 − 0.135

d) 0.01 + 0.02

To add or subtract decimals without using fractions:

Step 1: Line up the decimal points. Write zeros to the right of the last digit so all numbers will have the same number of decimal digits.

Step 2: Add or subtract the decimals as if they were whole numbers. Place the decimal point in the answer under the other decimal points.

Example: 1.45 − 0.924

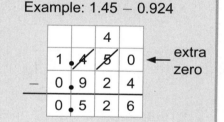

← extra zero

3. Add or subtract.

a) 0.145 + 1.237

b) 2.35 − 1.18

c) 13.45 − 9.237

d) 5.06 + 13.573

4. Jane spent $8.45 on lunch and paid with a $20 bill. How much is her change?

To multiply numbers with decimals, multiply as if they were whole numbers, and then place the decimal point so that there will be the same number of decimal digits.

Example: $1.34 \times 2 = \dfrac{134}{100} \times 2 = \dfrac{268}{100} = 2.68$

5. Multiply.

a) 2.34 × 3

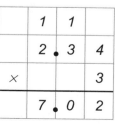

b) 4.125 × 2

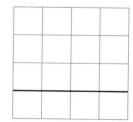

c) 12.37 × 3

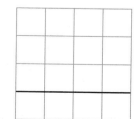

d) 8.45 × 9

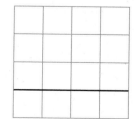

To multiply a decimal by a decimal:

Example: $1.3 \times 0.12 = \dfrac{13}{10} \times \dfrac{12}{100} = \dfrac{156}{1,000} = 0.156$

Step 1: Multiply the decimals as if they were whole numbers.

$13 \times 12 = 156$

Step 2: Count the digits after the decimal points, then find the total number of decimal digits.

1.3 has **1** digit after the decimal point. 0.12 has **2** digits after the decimal point. **1 + 2 = 3**

Step 3: Shift the decimal point left that many places.

0.156. So $1.3 \times 0.12 = 0.156$

6. Multiply.

a) 2.34×1.2

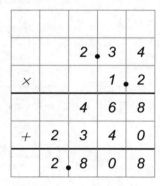

b) 32.1×2.4

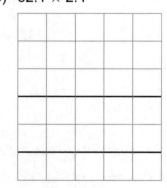

c) 1.345×2.9

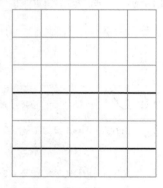

 d) 9.84×0.1

e) 9.84×0.01

f) 42.35×21.02

7. To convert temperatures in degrees Celsius to degrees Fahrenheit, multiply the Celsius temperature by 1.8 and add 32. Convert 23.5 degrees Celsius into degrees Fahrenheit.

8. The state tax in New York State is found by multiplying the retail price by 0.075. Find the tax on a sofa with a price tag of $240.

REMINDER: To multiply a decimal by 10, move the decimal point 1 place to the right.
To multiply a decimal by 100, move the decimal point 2 places to the right.

Examples: $2.35 \times 10 = 23.5$ $3.146 \times 100 = 314.6$ $23 \times 10 = 23.0 \times 10 = 230.0$

9. Multiply mentally.

a) 54.67×10

b) 0.345×100

c) $2.76 \times 1,000$

d) 0.002×100

e) $0.034 \times 1,000$

f) 29.38×10

g) 0.0098×100

h) $4.82 \times 1,000$

You can write division as a fraction. You can also multiply the numerator and the denominator by the same number to make an equivalent fraction.

To divide by a decimal, multiply both the dividend and the divisor by the power of 10 that makes the divisor a **whole number**.

Example:

$$0.23\overline{)0.828} \rightarrow \frac{0.828 \times 100}{0.23 \times 100}$$

$$0.23\overline{)0.828} \rightarrow 23\overline{)82.8}$$

10. Write an equivalent division question so that the divisor is a whole number.

a) $0.3\overline{)0.243}$
b) $0.12\overline{)21.6}$
c) $0.08\overline{)0.0984}$
d) $4.2\overline{)882}$

11. Write an equivalent division question so that the divisor is a whole number, and then divide. Place the decimal point in the quotient directly above the new decimal point in the dividend.

a) $0.5\overline{)1.15}$
b) $0.07\overline{)0.168}$
c) $0.23\overline{)9.43}$
d) $1.8\overline{)6.12}$

$5\overline{)11.5}$

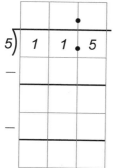

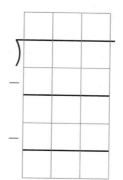

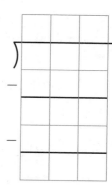

To change a fraction into a decimal:

Step 1: Write the numerator as a decimal.

Step 2: Divide the numerator by the denominator.

Step 3: Keep dividing until there is no remainder.

Example: $\frac{3}{4}$

$= 3.000 \div 4$

$$\begin{array}{r} 0.75 \\ 4\overline{)3.000} \\ -28\downarrow \\ \hline 20 \\ -20 \\ \hline 0 \end{array}$$

So $\frac{3}{4} = 0.75$

12. Write the fraction as a decimal.

a) $\frac{1}{4}$
b) $\frac{3}{8}$
c) $\frac{17}{20}$
d) $\frac{18}{25}$

13. If 0.75 grams of gold costs $80.31, what is the cost of one gram of gold?

14. In baseball, a batting average is calculated by dividing the number of hits by the number of times at bat. Joey Slugger had 22 hits in 80 at bats. What is his batting average?

11. Integers

Integers include positive whole numbers, negative whole numbers, and zero.

An integer is any of the numbers: ..., −4, −3, −2, −1, 0, +1, +2, +3, +4, ...

You can represent integers on a number line. Positive numbers do not need to have the + sign

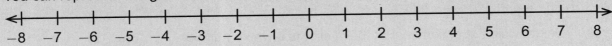

1. Label the integers on the number line with their letters.

U. −5   **E.** 3   **R.** 4   **N.** −7   **M.** −2   **B.** −1   **S.** +6

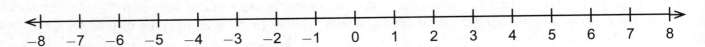

A number line shows how the numbers compare.

2 is **greater** than −3; 2 is farther to the **right** on the number line.   We write 2 > −3.

−5 is **less** than −1; −5 is farther to the **left** on the number line.   We write −5 < −1.

2. Circle the larger integer.

a) ⑤, −3   b) −2, 4   c) −3, −7   d) −8, 0

3. a) Circle the integers −5, 3, −7, 4, 0, and −1 on the number line.

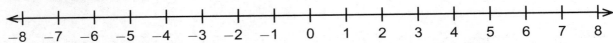

   b) Write the integers in order from least to greatest. _____ < _____ < _____ < _____ < _____ < _____

   c) Write the integers in order from greatest to least. _____ > _____ > _____ > _____ > _____ > _____

4. Write the integers −15, 23, 0, −8, −17, 14, and −1 from least to greatest.

   _____ < _____ < _____ < _____ < _____ < _____ < _____

Integers are used in many everyday situations to describe numbers that are compared to zero.

Examples: −30°C is 30 degrees below the temperature at which water freezes (0°C).

          +30,000 ft is 30,000 ft above sea level (0 ft).

5. Write an integer for the situation.

   a) A gain in weight of 10 lb. _____   b) A decrease of $235 in a bank account. _____

   c) A golf score that is 3 strokes below par. _____   d) A gain in the stock market of 250 points. _____

You can use (+) to represent (+1) and (−) to represent (−1).

Examples: (+)(+)(+) represents (+3). (−)(−) represents (−2).

6. Draw a diagram to represent the integer.

a) (−3)

b) (+2)

c) (−4)

d) (+5)

(−)(−)(−)

A gain of $1 (+1) followed by a loss of $1 (−1) is the same as no gain or loss. We write $(+1) + (−1) = 0$.

You can represent $(+1) + (−1)$ with a diagram: (+)(−)

To add $(+3) + (−5)$:

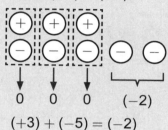

$(+3) + (−5) = (−2)$

To add $(+5) + (−2)$:

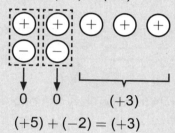

$(+5) + (−2) = (+3)$

7. Use a diagram to add the integers.

a) $(+4) + (−2)$

b) $(+3) + (−7)$

c) $(+4) + (+2)$

d) $(−4) + (−2)$

To add integers without a diagram, think of a contest between the positives and negatives. Who won the contest: the positives or the negatives? By how many did they win?

Question	Who Won?	By How Many?	Answer
$(+3) + (−5)$	negatives	2	$(+3) + (−5) = (−2)$
$(+7) + (−4)$	positives	3	$(+7) + (−4) = (+3)$
$(−3) + (−2)$	negatives	5	$(−3) + (−2) = (−5)$

8. Add without using a diagram.

a) $(+7) + (−2) =$

b) $(−8) + (+5) =$

c) $(−6) + (−3) =$

d) $(−5) + (−4) =$

e) $(+5) + (+4) =$

f) $(−3) + (−6) =$

g) $(−3) + (−3) =$

h) $(+6) + (−8) =$

9. Add without using a diagram.

a) $(+5) + (−2) + (−4) =$

b) $(−3) + (−2) + (+6) =$

c) $(+8) + (−3) + (+4) =$

d) $(−3) + (−5) + (+6) =$

e) $(−1) + (−4) + (−3) =$

f) $(+3) + (−5) + (+2) =$

To show how we subtract integers, we remove the integers from the diagram. If necessary, we can add zeros in the form of ⊕ ⊖ so there will be enough positives or negatives to remove.

(+5) − (+2) = (+3)

⊕ ⊕ ⊕ [⊕ ⊕] ↗

(+3) − (−2) = (+5)

⊕ ⊕ ⊕ ⊕ ⊕

[⊖ ⊖] ↗
↑ ↑

Add 2 groups of zero so we can take away 2 negatives

(−3) − (+3) = (−6)

⊖ ⊖ ⊖ [⊕ ⊕ ⊕] ↗

⊖ ⊖ ⊖
↑ ↑ ↑

Add 3 groups of zero so we can take away 3 positives

10. Use a diagram to subtract the integers.

a) (+4) − (+5) b) (−2) − (+3) c) (−3) − (−2) d) (−3) − (−4)

Opposite integers are the same distance from 0, but on opposite sides of 0 on the number line.

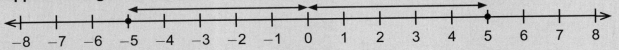

Example: −5 and 5 are both 5 units from 0. They are opposite integers.

11. Find the opposite integer.

a) (−3) _____ b) (+4) _____ c) (+8) _____ d) (−12) _____

Subtracting an integer is the same as adding its opposite integer.

(+3) − (−2) = (+3) + (+2)

⊕ ⊕ ⊕ ⊕ ⊕

[⊖ ⊖]
↑ ↑

Adding 2 zeros in the form of (+1) + (−1) twice and then taking away the 2 negatives is the same as adding (+2).

(−3) − (+3) = (−3) + (−3)

⊖ ⊖ ⊖ [⊕ ⊕ ⊕] ↗

⊖ ⊖ ⊖
↑ ↑ ↑

Adding 3 zeros in the form of (+1) + (−1) each and then taking away the 3 positives is the same as adding (−3).

12. Subtract by adding the opposite integer.

a) (+3) − (−4) b) (−4) − (+2) c) (+7) − (−3) d) (−3) − (−5)

= (+3) + (+4) = (−4) + (−2)

= (+7) = (−6)

e) (+2) − (+8) f) (−6) − (−2) g) (−1) − (+5) h) (−4) − (−7)

13. After the bank accidentally charged Rachel $5 in service fees, her account balance was $45. The bank corrected the mistake and returned the money to Rachel's account. Use integer subtraction to show that her balance is now $50.

12. Operations with Integers

Multiplication is a short form for addition. Multiplication is also commutative.

$(+3) \times (-2)$

$= (-2) + (-2) + (-2)$ ◄—— add (-2)
                                three times

$= (-6)$

$(-2) \times (+3)$

$= (+3) \times (-2)$ ◄—— commutative
                              property

$= (-6)$

To multiply integers $(+) \times (-) = (-)$
with opposite signs: $(-) \times (+) = (-)$

So $(+3) \times (-2) = (-6)$ and $(-2) \times (+3) = (-6)$. Both are the opposite of $3 \times 2 = 6$.

1. Multiply.

a) $(+3) \times (-4)$

= _____

b) $(-5) \times (+6)$

= _____

c) $(-8) \times (+7)$

= _____

d) $(+2) \times (-9)$

= _____

e) $(+2) \times (-10)$

= _____

f) $(-9) \times (+9)$

= _____

g) $(-8) \times (+8)$

= _____

h) $(-2) \times 0$

= _____

2. a) Continue the patterns to complete the charts.

i)

First Integer	Second Integer	Product
(+4)	(−3)	(−12)
(+3)	(−3)	(−9)
(+2)	(−3)	
(+1)	(−3)	
	(−3)	
	(−3)	
	(−3)	
	(−3)	
	(−3)	

ii)

First Integer	Second Integer	Product
(+4)	(−2)	(−8)
(+3)	(−2)	(−6)
(+2)	(−2)	
(+1)	(−2)	
	(−2)	
	(−2)	
	(−2)	
	(−2)	
	(−2)	

b) What is the sign of the product when one integer is negative and the other integer is positive? _____

c) What is the sign of the product when the first and second integers are both negative?

_____

A negative integer multiplied by a negative integer is a positive integer. Example: $(-3) \times (-4) = (+12)$

3. Multiply.

a) $(-3) \times (-5)$

b) $(-5) \times (-2)$

c) $(-2) \times (-7)$

= _____

= _____

= _____

The fact family for $3 \times 4 = 12$ includes $4 \times 3 = 12$, $12 \div 4 = 3$, and $12 \div 3 = 4$.

4. Write the other members of the fact family.

a) $(+5) \times (-2) = (-10)$

b) $(-7) \times (+3) = (-21)$

c) $(-4) \times (-5) = (+20)$

   $(-2) \times (+5) = (-10)$

   _____

   _____

   $(-10) \div (+5) = (-2)$

   _____

   _____

   $(-10) \div (-2) = (+5)$

   _____

   _____

5. Use your answers from Question 4 to fill in the blank.

a) When a negative integer is divided by a positive integer, the answer is _____.

b) When a positive integer is divided by a negative integer, the answer is _____.

c) When a negative integer is divided by a negative integer, the answer is _____.

To multiply or divide integers:

- if the signs are the same, the answer is positive. $(+)(+) = (+)$ $(-)(-) = (+)$
- if the signs are different, the answer is negative. $(+)(-) = (-)$ $(-)(+) = (-)$

6. Multiply or divide.

a) $(-3) \times (+4)$

b) $(+5) \times (-3)$

c) $(-8) \times (-6)$

= _____

= _____

= _____

d) $(+3) \times (+7)$

e) $(-24) \div (-6)$

f) $(-9) \div (+9)$

= _____

= _____

= _____

g) $(+27) \div (-3)$

h) $(+5) \div (-5)$

i) $0 \times (+5)$

= _____

= _____

= _____

j) $0 \times (-5)$

k) $0 \div (+7)$

l) $0 \div (-7)$

= _____

= _____

= _____

To make expressions easier to read, you should …

- write positive numbers without brackets or signs.
- rewrite subtracting an integer as adding the opposite integer.
- use brackets around negative integers if two signs are written together.

$(+3) = 3$

$3 - 5 = 3 + (-5)$

$3 + -5 = 3 + (-5)$

7. Rewrite the expression to use only addition.

a) $4 - 6$

$= 4 + (-6)$

b) $-3 - 2$

c) $4 - 7$

d) $-7 - (-2)$

e) $4 - 5 + 3 - 6$

f) $7 + 9 - 4 - 2$

g) $-3 - 4 + 6 - 2$

h) $-2 - 3 - 4$

8. Rewrite the expression to use only addition, and then calculate.

a) $5 - 8$

$= 5 + (-8)$

$= -3$

b) $-3 - 4$

c) $6 - (-8)$

d) $-2 - (-5)$

e) $6 - 8 - 3$

f) $-2 + 4 - 7$

g) $-2 - 6 - 7$

h) $6 - 4 + 3$

9. Calculate by adding the positive numbers and the negative numbers separately.

a) $3 - 6 - 4 + 8$

$= 3 + 8 + (-6) + (-4)$

$= 11 + (-10)$

$= 1$

b) $-2 + 6 - 8 + 9$

c) $4 - 6 + 5 - 3 - 8 + 9$

d) $-6 + 5 - 3 - 2 + 7$

10. Find the value of the expression. Remember to follow the correct order of operations.

a) $3 - 5 \times (-2)$

$= 3 + (-5)(-2)$

$= 3 + 10$

$= 13$

b) $-10 + 2 \times 3 \times (-4)$

c) $-24 \div (-8) + (-2) \times (-3)$

d) $14 - 21 \div (-3)$

e) $(-5 + 2) \times (-3 - 4)$

f) $-5 \times 2 - 12 \div (-4)$

11. Liquid nitrogen freezes at −346°F. A beaker containing liquid nitrogen at a temperature of −334°F is being cooled at the rate of 2°F per minute. Will it be frozen after 5 minutes?

_____

_____

REMINDER: You can write a fraction as a division. Example: $\dfrac{6}{2} = 6 \div 2$

12. a) Rewrite the fraction as a division statement and calculate the answer.

i) $\dfrac{-6}{2}$

$= (-6) \div 2$

$= (-3)$

ii) $\dfrac{6}{-2}$

iii) $-\left(\dfrac{6}{2}\right)$

iv) $\dfrac{-6}{-2}$

b) What do you notice about your answers to i) to iii), above? Is your answer to part iv) the same?

_____

When a fraction has a single negative sign, you can place the sign in the numerator, in the denominator, or outside the fraction.

Example: $\dfrac{-10}{2} = \dfrac{10}{-2} = -\dfrac{10}{2} = -5$

13. Calculate.

a) $\dfrac{5}{7} + \dfrac{3}{-7}$

$= \dfrac{5}{7} + \dfrac{-3}{7}$

$= \dfrac{2}{7}$

b) $\dfrac{-3}{5} + \dfrac{1}{-5}$

c) $-\dfrac{1}{8} + \dfrac{7}{8}$

d) $\dfrac{1}{4} - \dfrac{1}{-4}$

14. Find a common denominator and then calculate.

a) $\dfrac{5}{6} + \dfrac{1}{-8}$

$= \dfrac{5}{6} + \dfrac{-1}{8}$

$= \dfrac{20}{24} + \dfrac{-3}{24}$

$= \dfrac{17}{24}$

b) $\dfrac{-3}{4} + \dfrac{5}{-6}$

c) $\dfrac{7}{-9} - \dfrac{1}{-6}$

d) $\dfrac{-7}{10} - \dfrac{4}{-15}$

13. Powers Review

> A **power** is a short form for repeated **multiplication**.
>
> Example: $3^4 = 3 \times 3 \times 3 \times 3$
>
> The power 3^4 means multiply 3 four times.
>
> The exponent tells you how many times to multiply the base.

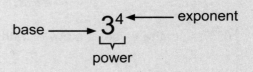

1. Write the base and the exponent for the power.

   a) 2^5 base = ___2___

      exponent = ___5___

   b) 4^3 base = _____

      exponent = _____

   c) 7^2 base = _____

      exponent = _____

2. Write the power as a product.

   a) $2^4 = 2 \times 2 \times 2 \times 2$

   b) $8^3 =$

   c) $10^4 =$

   d) $7^2 =$

   e) $10^3 =$

   f) $0^2 =$

3. Write the product as a power.

   a) $5 \times 5 \times 5 \times 5 = 5^4$

   b) $9 \times 9 \times 9 =$

   c) $10 \times 10 =$

   d) $0 \times 0 \times 0 =$

   e) $(-1) \times (-1) \times (-1) =$

   f) $2 \times 2 \times 2 \times 2 \times 2 \times 2 =$

4. Evaluate the power.

   a) 2^3

      $= 2 \times 2 \times 2$

      $= 8$

   b) 3^2

   c) 6^3

   d) $(-2)^3$

   e) 0^4

   f) $\left(\dfrac{1}{2}\right)^3$

   g) 10^2

   h) 10^3

   Bonus ▶ 10^6

5. a) Evaluate the power.

      i) $1^3 =$ _____

      ii) $1^5 =$ _____

      iii) $1^{10} =$ _____

      Bonus ▶ $1^{75} =$ _____

   b) Predict the value of any power with the base 1. _____

6. a) Evaluate the power.

  i) $8^1 =$ _____   ii) $3^1 =$ _____   iii) $9^1 =$ _____   **Bonus ▶** $235^1 =$ _____

  b) Predict the value of a power with any base to the exponent 1. _____

7. Write the number as a power.

  a) $8 = \underline{8^1}$ b) $5 =$ _____   c) $(-3) =$ _____   d) $\left(\dfrac{1}{2}\right) =$ _____

Remember the order of operations with powers: evaluate the power before multiplying or dividing.

Example: $3 \times 2^4 = 3 \times (2 \times 2 \times 2 \times 2)$
$$= 3 \times 16$$
$$= 48$$

---

8. Evaluate the power, then multiply.

  a) 2×5^2 b) 3×6^2 c) 4×10^3 d) 2.8×10^2

  $= 2 \times 25$

  $= 50$

9. Evaluate the expression. Use the standard order of operations.

  a) $3^2 + 4^2$ b) $17 - 2^3$ c) $2^4 \times 3^2$ d) $10^4 \div 10^3$

  $= 9 + 16$

  $= 25$

  e) $3 + 5^2$ f) $(3 + 5)^2$ g) $\dfrac{8^2}{2^4}$ h) $(5 \times 2)^3$

10. A **scientific calculator** has a button to evaluate powers. The example shows the buttons to press to evaluate powers.

  Use a scientific calculator to evaluate the power.

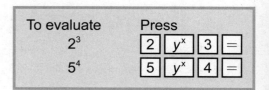

To evaluate	Press
2^3	$\boxed{2}\;\boxed{y^x}\;\boxed{3}\;\boxed{=}$
5^4	$\boxed{5}\;\boxed{y^x}\;\boxed{4}\;\boxed{=}$

  a) $2^5 =$ _____   b) $9^3 =$ _____   c) $6^4 =$ _____   d) $2^{10} =$ _____

11. Ben thinks that $4^3 = 12$ and $8^2 = 16$. Is he correct? Explain your answer.

_____

_____

14. Product of Powers

1. Write each power as a product. How many times do you multiply each base?

  a) $2^3 \times 5^4$ b) $7^2 \times 9^3$ c) $4^3 \times 6^5$

   $= 2 \times 2 \times 2 \times 5 \times 5 \times 5 \times 5$

   __3__ times   __4__ times   _____ times   _____ times   _____ times   _____ times

  d) $3^2 \times 8^3$ e) $6^2 \times 7^2$ f) $10^3 \times 2^4$

   _____ times   _____ times   _____ times   _____ times   _____ times   _____ times

2. How many times do you multiply each base? Write the expression as a product of powers.

  a) $2 \times 2 \times 2 \times 2 \times 7 \times 7 \times 7$ b) $5 \times 5 \times 6 \times 6 \times 6$ c) $8 \times 8 \times 8 \times 9 \times 9 \times 9 \times 9$

   __4__ times   __3__ times   _____ times   _____ times   _____ times   _____ times

   $= 2^4 \times 7^3$ $=$ $=$

  d) $3 \times 3 \times 6 \times 6 \times 6 \times 6$ e) $4 \times 4 \times 4 \times 9 \times 9 \times 9$ f) $5 \times 5 \times 5 \times 5 \times 5 \times 4 \times 4$

   _____ times   _____ times   _____ times   _____ times   _____ times   _____ times

   $=$ $=$ $=$

3. Write each power as a product. Then write the final product as a single power.

  a) $2^3 \times 2^4$ b) $5^4 \times 5^2$ c) $9^2 \times 9^6$

   $= (2 \times 2 \times 2) \times (2 \times 2 \times 2 \times 2)$

   $= 2 \times 2 \times 2 \times 2 \times 2 \times 2 \times 2$

   $= 2^7$

  d) $7^5 \times 7^4$ e) $8^3 \times 8^2$ f) $2^7 \times 2^3$

4. a) Use your answers from Question 3 to complete the table.

Question	$2^3 \times 2^4$	$5^4 \times 5^2$	$9^2 \times 9^6$	$7^5 \times 7^4$	$8^3 \times 8^2$	$2^7 \times 2^3$
Answer	2^7					

b) Look at the exponents in each question and answer in the table. How can you predict the exponent in the answer using only the exponents in the question?

_____

To multiply powers with the same base, keep the base and add the exponents.

Example: $2^3 \times 2^4$
$= 2^{3+4}$
$= 2^7$

5. Write the product as a single power by keeping the base and adding the exponents.

a) $5^3 \times 5^4$

$= 5^{3+4}$

$= 5^7$

b) $3^2 \times 3^4$

c) $2^5 \times 2^4$

d) $3^5 \times 3^3$

e) $7^3 \times 7^5$

f) $9^7 \times 9^3$

To check that $2^3 \times 2^4 = 2^7$, evaluate each side of the equation separately.

Left Side: $2^3 \times 2^4 = 8 \times 16 = 128$ **Right Side:** $2^7 = 2 \times 2 \times 2 \times 2 \times 2 \times 2 \times 2 = 128$

Since the left side equals the right side, $2^3 \times 2^4 = 2^7$.

6. Evaluate each side of the equation separately to check that the equation is true.

a) $3^2 \times 3^3 = 3^5$

b) $2^4 \times 2^2 = 2^6$

c) $10^3 \times 10^4 = 10^7$

7. Mona thinks that $2^3 \times 5^2 = 10^5$. Evaluate each side of the equation separately to check. When multiplying powers, what must be true about the bases before you can add the exponents?

8. Write the product as a single power by keeping the base and adding the exponents.

a) $5^6 \times 5$

$= 5^6 \times 5^1$

$= 5^7$

b) $8^4 \times 8$

c) $7^9 \times 7$

d) 4×4^6

e) 8×8^5

f) 10×10^8

9. Write the product as a single power.

a) $(5^6 \times 5^2) \times 5^3$

$= 5^8 \times 5^3$

$= 5^{11}$

b) $(3^4 \times 3^5) \times 3^6$

c) $2^4 \times (2^5 \times 2^3)$

d) $(6^4 \times 6^2) \times (6^3 \times 6^5)$

e) $(9^3 \times 9) \times (9^2 \times 9^7)$

f) $(5^3 \times 5 \times 5^4) \times 5^6$

10. Write the product of powers as a single power.

a) $2^3 \times 2^5 \times 2^4$

$= 2^{3+5+4}$

$= 2^{12}$

b) $10^3 \times 10^4 \times 10$

c) $(-3)^6 \times (-3) \times (-3)^2$

d) $10 \times 10^7 \times 10$

e) $\left(\dfrac{1}{2}\right)^2 \times \left(\dfrac{1}{2}\right)^3 \times \left(\dfrac{1}{2}\right)$

f) $(0.2)^3 \times (0.2) \times (0.2)^2$

11. Multiply powers with the same base.

a) $2^3 \times 2^5 \times 3^4 \times 3^2$

$= 2^{3+5} \times 3^{4+2}$

$= 2^8 \times 3^6$

b) $4^7 \times 4^2 \times 6^5 \times 6^7$

c) $3^5 \times 8^2 \times 3^4 \times 8^3$

15. Quotient of Powers

A fraction with a product in the numerator and in the denominator can be written as a product of separate fractions.

Example: $\dfrac{4 \times 3}{7 \times 5} = \dfrac{4}{7} \times \dfrac{3}{5}$

1. Write the fraction as a product of separate fractions.

   a) $\dfrac{5 \times 7}{2 \times 3} =$

   b) $\dfrac{6 \times 2}{5 \times 11} =$

   c) $\dfrac{3 \times 2}{4 \times 2} =$

2. Write the fraction as a product of separate fractions. Multiply by 1 to make the number of factors in the numerator and the denominator the same.

   a) $\dfrac{5 \times 6 \times 8}{2 \times 3}$

   $= \dfrac{5 \times 6 \times 8}{1 \times 2 \times 3}$

   $= \dfrac{5}{1} \times \dfrac{6}{2} \times \dfrac{8}{3}$

   b) $\dfrac{4 \times 7 \times 6 \times 8}{8 \times 9}$

   $= \dfrac{4 \times 7 \times 6 \times 8}{1 \times 1 \times 8 \times 9}$

   c) $\dfrac{3 \times 2 \times 5 \times 7 \times 6}{8 \times 9}$

   d) $\dfrac{3 \times 2 \times 7 \times 5}{4 \times 9}$

   e) $\dfrac{8 \times 5}{4}$

   f) $\dfrac{3 \times 2 \times 7 \times 5 \times 9}{6}$

3. Write the powers as products and then as the product of separate fractions. Multiply by 1 to make the number of factors in the numerator and the denominator the same.

   a) $\dfrac{2^5}{2^3}$

   $= \dfrac{2 \times 2 \times 2 \times 2 \times 2}{2 \times 2 \times 2}$

   $= \dfrac{2 \times 2 \times 2 \times 2 \times 2}{1 \times 1 \times 2 \times 2 \times 2}$

   $= \dfrac{2}{1} \times \dfrac{2}{1} \times \dfrac{2}{2} \times \dfrac{2}{2} \times \dfrac{2}{2}$

   b) $\dfrac{3^5}{3^2}$

   c) $\dfrac{7^6}{7^2}$

   d) $\dfrac{8^5}{8^2}$

   e) $\dfrac{9^7}{9^3}$

   f) $\dfrac{10^6}{10^2}$

REMINDER: A fraction with the same numerator and denominator is equal to 1. Example: $\frac{5}{5} = 1$

4. Evaluate.

a) $\dfrac{8}{8} =$

b) $\dfrac{10}{10} =$

c) $\dfrac{45}{45} =$

$\dfrac{4^5}{4^2}$ is called a **quotient of powers**. To divide, write the numerator and denominator as products.

$\dfrac{4^5}{4^2} = \dfrac{4 \times 4 \times 4 \times 4 \times 4}{4 \times 4}$ ←——— multiply four 5 times

←——— multiply four 2 times

$= \dfrac{4 \times 4 \times 4 \times 4 \times 4}{1 \times 1 \times 1 \times 4 \times 4}$

$= \left(\dfrac{4}{1}\right) \times \dfrac{4}{1} \times \dfrac{4}{1} \times \dfrac{4}{4} \times \left(\dfrac{4}{4}\right)$ ←——— $\dfrac{4}{1} = 4$ $\dfrac{4}{4} = 1$

$= 4 \times 4 \times 4 \times 1 \times 1$ ←——— multiply four 3 times

$= 4^3$

Shortcut:

There are 3 more 4s in the numerator than in the denominator, so $\dfrac{4^5}{4^2} = 4^3$.

5. Find how many more times the base appears in the numerator, then write as a single power.

a) $\dfrac{6^5}{6^3}$

$= \dfrac{6 \times 6 \times 6 \times 6 \times 6}{6 \times 6 \times 6}$

$= 6 \times 6$

$= 6^2$

b) $\dfrac{8^4}{8^2}$

c) $\dfrac{2^7}{2^4}$

d) $\dfrac{10^6}{10^4}$

e) $\dfrac{3^5}{3^2}$

f) $\dfrac{7^6}{7^2}$

To divide powers with the same base, keep the base and subtract the exponents.

$6^7 \div 6^4$
$= 6^{7-4}$
$= 6^3$

or

$\dfrac{6^7}{6^4} = 6^{7-4}$
$= 6^3$

6. Divide by keeping the base and subtracting the exponents.

a) $\dfrac{2^7}{2^4} = 2^{7-4} = 2^3$

b) $\dfrac{7^9}{7^3} =$

c) $4^9 \div 4^7 =$

d) $\dfrac{8^6}{8^2} =$

e) $10^7 \div 10^3 =$

f) $\dfrac{(-2)^4}{(-2)^2} =$

7. Divide, then evaluate the power.

a) $\dfrac{5^8}{5^6} = 5^2 = 25$

b) $6^7 \div 6^5 =$

c) $\dfrac{2^9}{2^6} =$

d) $\dfrac{10^8}{10^5} =$

e) $\dfrac{(-1)^7}{(-1)^5} =$

Bonus ▶ $\dfrac{4^{187}}{4^{184}} =$

8. Write the quotient as a single power. Hint: $2 = 2^1$.

a) $\dfrac{2^7}{2} = 2^{7-1} = 2^6$

b) $\dfrac{3^5}{3} =$

c) $\dfrac{5^9}{5} =$

d) $\dfrac{4^{11}}{4} =$

e) $\dfrac{(-3)^6}{(-3)} =$

Bonus ▶ $\dfrac{123^{95}}{123} =$

> To check that $2^5 \div 2^2 = 2^3$, evaluate each side of the equation separately.
>
> **Left side:** $2^5 \div 2^2 = 32 \div 4 = 8$ **Right side:** $2^3 = 2 \times 2 \times 2 = 8$
>
> Since the left side equals the right side, $2^5 \div 2^2 = 2^3$.

9. Evaluate each side separately to check that the equation is true.

a) $3^5 \div 3^3 = 3^2$

b) $4^4 \div 4^3 = 4^1$

c) $10^6 \div 10^4 = 10^2$

10. David thinks that $10^5 \div 5^2 = 2^3$. Evaluate each side of the equation separately to check. When dividing powers, what must be true about the bases before you can subtract the exponents?

> For some questions, you will need to use the rules for multiplying powers and dividing powers. Use the rules to rewrite the expression as a single power.
>
> $2^6 \times 2^3 \div 2^4$ ◀—— multiplying powers with the same base
>
> $= 2^9 \div 2^4$ ◀—— dividing powers with the same base
>
> $= 2^5$

11. Rewrite the expression as a single power. Hint: Operations in brackets are done first.

a) $3^5 \times 3^7 \div 3^8$

$= 3^{12} \div 3^8$

$= 3^4$

b) $5^7 \times 5^6 \div 5^{11}$

c) $10^7 \times 10^4 \div 10^8$

d) $6^8 \div (6^3 \times 6^2)$

e) $7^{10} \div (7^3 \times 7^2)$

f) $(4^8 \times 4^4) \div (4^3 \times 4^6)$

16. Zero and Negative Exponents

> **REMINDER:** A fraction with the same numerator and denominator is equal to 1. Example: $\dfrac{5}{5} = 1$

1. Evaluate the fraction.

a) $\dfrac{2^4}{2^4} = \dfrac{16}{16} = 1$

b) $\dfrac{3^2}{3^2} =$

c) $\dfrac{4^3}{4^3} =$

d) $\dfrac{5^2}{5^2} =$

e) $\dfrac{2^6}{2^6} =$

f) $\dfrac{10^3}{10^3} =$

> **REMINDER:** To divide powers with the same base, keep the base and subtract the exponents.
>
> Example: $\dfrac{2^7}{2^3} = 2^4$

2. Divide by keeping the base and subtracting the exponents.

a) $\dfrac{2^4}{2^4} = 2^{4-4} = 2^0$

b) $\dfrac{3^2}{3^2} =$

c) $\dfrac{4^3}{4^3} =$

d) $\dfrac{5^2}{5^2} =$

e) $\dfrac{2^6}{2^6} =$

f) $\dfrac{10^3}{10^3} =$

3. a) In Question 1, what was the answer each time? _____

b) In Question 2, what was the exponent in the answer each time? _____

A power with the exponent zero has the value 1.   Example: $2^0 = 1$

4. Find the value of the power.

a) $4^0 =$ _____

b) $9^0 =$ _____

c) $10^0 =$ _____

d) $(-8)^0 =$ _____

e) $\left(\dfrac{3}{5}\right)^0 =$ _____

Bonus ▶ $1{,}237^0 =$ _____

5. Evaluate the expression. Use the correct order of operations.

a) $2^0 + 2^3 \times 3^2$

$= 1 + 8 \times 9$

$= 1 + 72$

$= 73$

b) $3^2 + 5^2 \div 4^0$

c) $\dfrac{5^3}{5^3} + \dfrac{5^3}{5}$

d) $(8^2 - 4^0) \div (5 \times 2^2 + 7^0)$

e) $(5^2)^0$

f) $(2 + 3 \times 5)^0$

6. Write the quotient of powers as a product of fractions. Multiply by 1 to make the number of factors in the numerator and denominator the same.

a) $\dfrac{2^3}{2^5}$

b) $\dfrac{3^3}{3^7}$

c) $\dfrac{4^3}{4^6}$

$= \dfrac{2 \times 2 \times 2}{2 \times 2 \times 2 \times 2 \times 2}$

$= \dfrac{1 \times 1 \times 2 \times 2 \times 2}{2 \times 2 \times 2 \times 2 \times 2}$

$= \dfrac{1}{2} \times \dfrac{1}{2} \times \dfrac{2}{2} \times \dfrac{2}{2} \times \dfrac{2}{2}$

d) $\dfrac{7^2}{7^6}$

e) $\dfrac{9^4}{9^5}$

f) $\dfrac{10^4}{10^6}$

To divide $\dfrac{4^2}{4^5}$, write the numerator and denominator as a product.

$\dfrac{4^2}{4^5} = \dfrac{4 \times 4}{4 \times 4 \times 4 \times 4 \times 4}$ ⟵ multiply four 2 times
⟵ multiply four 5 times

$= \dfrac{1 \times 1 \times 1 \times 4 \times 4}{4 \times 4 \times 4 \times 4 \times 4}$

$= \dfrac{1}{4} \times \dfrac{1}{4} \times \dfrac{1}{4} \times \left(\dfrac{4}{4}\right) \times \left(\dfrac{4}{4}\right)$ ⟵ $\dfrac{4}{4} = 1$

$= \dfrac{1}{4 \times 4 \times 4}$ ⟵ multiply four 3 times

$= \dfrac{1}{4^3}$

Shortcut:

There are 3 more 4s in the denominator than in the numerator, so $\dfrac{4^2}{4^5} = \dfrac{1}{4^3}$.

7. Find how many more times the base appears in the denominator, and then write as a single power.

a) $\dfrac{8^3}{8^5}$

b) $\dfrac{6^3}{6^7}$

c) $\dfrac{3^2}{3^6}$

$= \dfrac{8 \times 8 \times 8}{8 \times 8 \times 8 \times 8 \times 8}$ multiply 3 times
multiply 5 times

$= \dfrac{1}{8 \times 8}$ 2 more 8s in the denominator

$= \dfrac{1}{8^2}$

d) $\dfrac{10^2}{10^7}$

e) $\dfrac{9^2}{9^8}$

f) $\dfrac{4^5}{4^7}$

Remember: When dividing powers with the same base, keep the base and subtract the exponents.

But $\dfrac{2^3}{2^7} = \dfrac{1}{2^4}$ because there are 4 more 2s being multiplied in the denominator.

Example: $\dfrac{2^3}{2^7} = 2^{3-7} = 2^{-4}$

$2^{-4} = \dfrac{1}{2^4}$

8. Write the power as a fraction with a positive exponent in the denominator.

a) $2^{-3} = \dfrac{1}{2^3}$

b) $8^{-5} = \dfrac{1}{\underline{}}$

c) $7^{-3} = \dfrac{1}{\underline{}}$

d) $9^{-8} =$

e) $10^{-2} =$

f) $(-3)^{-2} =$

9. Write the fraction as a power with a negative exponent.

a) $\dfrac{1}{3^5} = 3^{-5}$

b) $\dfrac{1}{4^3} =$

c) $\dfrac{1}{6^4} =$

d) $\dfrac{1}{9^2} =$

e) $\dfrac{1}{10^4} =$

f) $\dfrac{1}{(-2)^6} =$

10. Evaluate the power by first writing it as a fraction.

a) 2^{-3}

$= \dfrac{1}{2^3}$

$= \dfrac{1}{8}$

b) 4^{-2}

c) 5^{-2}

d) 10^{-2}

e) 10^{-5}

f) $(-3)^{-4}$

11. Evaluate. If the answer has a negative exponent, rewrite it as a fraction.

a) $2^3 \times 2^{-6}$

$= 2^{3 + (-6)}$

$= 2^{-3}$

$= \dfrac{1}{2^3}$

$= \dfrac{1}{8}$

b) $3^8 \times 3^{-6}$

c) $4^3 \div 4^5$

d) $5^4 \times 5^3 \div 5^9$

e) $8^2 \div 8^6 \times 8^3$

f) $2^5 \div 2^7 \div 2^2$

17. Introduction to Scientific Notation

To multiply by a power of 10, move the decimal point to the right.	Examples: $2.8\ 3 \times 10$ = 28.3	$3.4\ 0 \times 100$ = 340

1. Evaluate the power, then multiply.

a) 2.4×10^2

   $= 2.4 \times 100$

   $= 240$

b) 4.56×10^3

c) 0.94×10^4

d) 0.345×10^3

e) 1.23×10^4

f) 0.094×10^5

To multiply by a power of 10 with a positive exponent, move the decimal point to the right as many places as the exponent.	Examples: $0.2\ 3\ 5\ 7 \times 10^3$ = 235.7

2. Multiply by moving the decimal point.

a) $0.345 \times 10^2 = 34.5$

b) $1.8193 \times 10^3 =$

c) $9.4 \times 10^2 =$

d) $82.3 \times 10^4 =$

e) $0.045 \times 10^2 =$

f) $0.0354 \times 10^5 =$

To divide by a power of 10, move the decimal point to the left.	Examples: $2\ 8\ 3.4 \div 10$ = 28.34	$7.48 \div 100$ = 0.0748

3. Evaluate the power first.

a) $2.48 \div 10^3$

   $= 2.48 \div 1,000$

   $= 0.00248$

b) $45.67 \div 10^2$

c) $94.87 \div 10^4$

d) $375.8 \div 10^2$

e) $1.23 \div 10^3$

f) $0.097 \div 10^4$

To divide by a power of 10 with a positive exponent, move the decimal point to the left as many places as the exponent.	Examples: $9\ 3.57 \div 10^3$ = 0.09357

4. Divide by moving the decimal point.

a) $82.3 \div 10^2 = 0.823$

b) $28.34 \div 10^3 =$

c) $9.4 \div 10^2 =$

d) $145.2 \div 10^3 =$

e) $0.25 \div 10^2 =$

f) $98.2 \div 10^3 =$

5. Use the grid to multiply or divide.

a) 2.38×10^3 | 0 | 2 . 3 | 8 | 0 | 0 | $= 2{,}380$

b) $3.58 \div 10^2$ | 0 | 0 | 3 . 5 | 8 | 0 | $= 0.0358$

c) 56.7×10^2 | 0 | 5 | 6 | 7 | 0 | 0 |

d) $45.9 \div 10^3$ | 0 | 0 | 4 | 5 | 9 | 0 |

e) $0.571 \div 10^1$ | 0 | 0 | 5 | 7 | 1 | 0 |

f) 0.056×10^4 | 0 | 0 | 5 | 6 | 0 | 0 |

g) 65.3×10^3 | 0 | 6 | 5 | 3 | 0 | 0 |

h) $467.8 \div 10^4$ | 0 | 4 | 6 | 7 | 8 | 0 |

REMINDER: To divide by a fraction, multiply by the reciprocal.

Examples: $6 \div \dfrac{3}{4} = 6 \times \dfrac{4}{3}$ $\qquad$ $5 \div 8 = 5 \times \dfrac{1}{8}$

---

6. Write the division statement using multiplication.

a) $2.3 \div 10$

$= 2.3 \times \dfrac{1}{10}$

b) $3.46 \div 100$

c) $42.687 \div 1{,}000$

7. Write the multiplication statement using division.

a) $5.6 \times \dfrac{1}{10}$

$= 5.6 \div 10$

b) $8.214 \times \dfrac{1}{100}$

c) $7.2 \times \dfrac{1}{1{,}000}$

8. Write the power of 10 as a fraction, then write the multiplication as a division.

a) 8.5×10^{-2}

$= 8.5 \times \dfrac{1}{10^2}$

$= 8.5 \div 10^2$

b) 8.419×10^{-3}

c) 1.27×10^{-5}

d) 6.73×10^{-1}

e) 4.25×10^{-2}

f) 7.1×10^{-3}

To multiply by a power of 10 with a negative exponent, move the decimal point left.

Example: $4.35 \times 10^{-2} = 4.35 \div 10^2$

$= 0.0435$

---

9. Multiply by moving the decimal point left.

a) $456.9 \times 10^{-2} = 4.569$

b) $93.4 \times 10^{-3} =$

c) $4.16 \times 10^{-1} =$

d) $32.96 \times 10^{-4} =$

e) $0.034 \times 10^{-2} =$

f) $5.873 \times 10^{-3} =$

Numbers that are very, very large or very, very small are difficult to work with. They may not even fit on your calculator!

To help deal with these numbers, we use **scientific notation**.

Example: 237,000

In scientific notation, numbers are written as the product of a decimal greater than or equal to 1 but less than 10 and a power of 10.

2.37×10^5

decimal number   power of 10

10. Circle the number if it is written in scientific notation.

a) 2.74×10^{23}

b) $3.14 + 10^{-5}$

c) 1.09×10^{-7}

d) $4.1 \div 10^3$

e) 8.7×10^{12}

f) 10.34×10^{-8}

To change from scientific notation to decimal form, move the decimal point …
- right if the power of 10 has a positive exponent.
- left if the power of 10 has a negative exponent.

Examples: $3.12 \times 10^4 = 3\,1,2\,0\,0.0$

$9.45 \times 10^{-3} = 0.0\,0\,9\,4\,5$

11. Change from scientific notation to decimal form.

a) $2.13 \times 10^4 = 21,300$

b) $8.74 \times 10^3 =$

c) $1.98 \times 10^5 =$

d) $7.2 \times 10^{-3} = 0.0072$

e) $5.146 \times 10^{-2} =$

f) $1.03 \times 10^{-4} =$

g) $9.4 \times 10^{-2} =$

h) $1.9 \times 10^3 =$

i) $2.03 \times 10^{-1} =$

12. A light year (the distance light can travel in 1 year) is approximately 9.5×10^{15} m. Write the distance in decimal form.

13. The mass of an electron is approximately 9.1×10^{-31} kg. What is the mass in decimal form?

14. a) The land area of Earth is approximately 1.49×10^8 km². What is the land area written in decimal form?

b) The water area of Earth is approximately 3.61×10^8 km². What is the water area written in decimal form?

c) How much greater is the water area than the land area of Earth in km²?

JUMP Math Accumula

18. Scientific Notation

> REMINDER: In scientific notation, numbers are written as the product of a decimal greater than or equal to 1 but less than 10 and a power of 10.
>
> Example: 8.1×10^{-4}
> decimal number   power of 10

1. Circle the number if it is written in scientific notation.

   a) 18.4×10^2

   b) 2.39×10^{-4}

   c) 0.37×10^8

   d) $534{,}000$

   e) 0.003456

   f) 1.07×10^1

To change from decimal form to scientific notation:

Step 1: Find the decimal number for the scientific notation.

a) Put the decimal point after the first non-zero digit.

b) Remove all zeroes at the beginning or end.

Examples:

$238{,}040{,}000$	0.006502
2.38040000	0006.502
2.3804	6.502

---

2. For the numbers in Question 1 that are not written in scientific notation, explain why.

3. The number has been changed to scientific notation. Find the decimal part of the answer.

   a) $260{,}300$

   $= \underline{\quad 2.603 \quad} \times 10^5$

   b) 0.004518

   $= \underline{\qquad\qquad} \times 10^{-3}$

   c) 65.3400

   $= \underline{\qquad\qquad} \times 10^1$

   d) 0.000005800

   $= \underline{\qquad\qquad} \times 10^{-6}$

   e) $1{,}000{,}457{,}000$

   $= \underline{\qquad\qquad} \times 10^9$

   f) 182.34

   $= \underline{\qquad\qquad} \times 10^2$

Step 2: Find the exponent for the power of 10.

a) Count the number of places between the decimal point and its original position.

b) If you counted to the right, the exponent is positive. If you counted to the left, the exponent is negative.

Examples:

2.3804 6.502

$238{,}040{,}000$ 0.006502

$= 2.3804 \times 10^8$ $= 6.502 \times 10^{-3}$

---

4. The number has been changed to scientific notation. Find the power of 10.

   a) $6{,}204$

   $= 6.204 \times \underline{\quad 10^3 \quad}$

   b) 0.00038

   $= 3.8 \times \underline{\qquad\qquad}$

   c) $92{,}000{,}000$

   $= 9.2 \times \underline{\qquad\qquad}$

   d) 0.5809

   $= 5.809 \times \underline{\qquad\qquad}$

   e) $3{,}060{,}010$

   $= 3.06001 \times \underline{\qquad\qquad}$

   f) 0.0854

   $= 8.54 \times \underline{\qquad\qquad}$

   g) 0.0074

   $= 7.4 \times \underline{\qquad\qquad}$

   h) 0.15

   $= 1.5 \times \underline{\qquad\qquad}$

   Bonus ▶ 9.8

   $= 9.8 \times \underline{\qquad\qquad}$

5. Perform **Step 1** and **Step 2** from the previous page to change the number to scientific notation.

   a) 248,000,000
      $= 2.48 \times 10^8$

   b) 0.00354
      $= 3.54 \times 10^{-3}$

   c) 91.356

   d) 123,987

   e) 0.0048

   f) 0.87

   g) 9.73

   Bonus ▶ 52,040,000,000,000,000,000

Scientific calculators have a button for scientific notation. The button might be $\boxed{EE}$ or $\boxed{EXP}$.
To change 1.56×10^3 to decimal form, press $\boxed{1.56}$ $\boxed{EE}$ $\boxed{3}$ $\boxed{=}$. The answer is 1,560.

---

6. Use a scientific calculator to change to decimal form.

   a) 6.57×10^8

   b) 9.41×10^{-1}

   c) 2.83×10^4

   d) 7.45×10^{-5}

   e) 1.052×10^4

   f) 6.04×10^{-3}

7. Change to scientific notation. Then use a calculator to check your answer by changing the number back to decimal form.

   a) 0.00624
      $= 6.24 \times 10^{-3}$

   b) 45,037,000

   c) 0.000034

   d) 15,803

   e) 0.205

   f) 38,000,000,000

8. A nanosecond is 0.000000001 s. How many seconds is a nanosecond written in scientific notation?

   _____

9. A picometer is a unit of length equal to 0.000000000001 m. What is the length written in scientific notation?

   _____

10. The star Mizar, in the Big Dipper, is approximately 741,000,000,000,000,000 m away from Earth. Write the distance in scientific notation.

   _____

JUMP Math Accumula

To compare numbers written in scientific notation:

- if the exponents are different, the number with the larger exponent is the larger number.
- if the exponents are the same, the number with the larger decimal is the larger number.

Examples:

$2.3 \times 10^{-2} > 9.4 \times 10^{-8}$

$9.2 \times 10^5 > 7.3 \times 10^5$

11. Circle the larger number.

a) 4.5×10^7 or 6.1×10^9

b) 1.73×10^4 or 5.1×10^4

c) 5.06×10^{-4} or 1.99×10^{-2}

12. Circle the smaller number.

a) 1.9×10^{-4} or 2.8×10^{-2}

b) 5.7×10^3 or 4.8×10^3

c) 3.9×10^{-2} or 9.38×10^{-1}

A number is not in scientific notation if the decimal part is not in the right range.

Example: 0.746×10^3

Not in the right range

13. Change to scientific notation by first changing to decimal form.

a) 0.746×10^3

$= 746$

$= 7.46 \times 10^2$

b) 834.6×10^{-4}

c) 0.024×10^{-3}

 d) $7,459.2 \times 10^{-2}$

 e) 0.0056×10^{-4}

f) 0.00056×10^7

If the decimal part is not in the right range, we can:

Step 1: Write the decimal part in scientific notation.

Step 2: Use the power rules to multiply the powers with the same base.

Example: 0.046×10^5

$(4.6 \times 10^{-2}) \times 10^5$

$= 4.6 \times 10^{-2+5}$

$= 4.6 \times 10^3$

14. Use the power rules to change to scientific notation.

a) 0.0813×10^7

$= (8.13 \times 10^{-2}) \times 10^7$

$= 8.13 \times 10^5$

b) 0.000172×10^{-3}

c) 536.12×10^{-5}

d) 482.1×10^4

e) 0.9×10^{-1}

f) 14.09×10^{-4}

19. Operations with Scientific Notation

To multiply or divide a number in scientific notation by a decimal, multiply or divide the decimals, and then multiply by the power of 10.

Examples: $(2.0 \times 10^3) \times 2.3$
$\qquad = (2.3 \times 2.0) \times 10^3$
$\qquad = 4.6 \times 10^3$

$\qquad\qquad (8.4 \times 10^5) \div 4.0$
$\qquad = (8.4 \div 4.0) \times 10^5$
$\qquad = 2.1 \times 10^5$

1. Multiply.

a) $(2.0 \times 10^4) \times 3.2$

b) $(3.0 \times 10^{-5}) \times 2.1$

c) $(3.0 \times 10^7) \times 1.2$

2. Divide.

a) $(6.3 \times 10^4) \div 3.0$

b) $(4.4 \times 10^{-3}) \div 4.0$

c) $(7.8 \times 10^{-3}) \div 2.0$

REMINDER: If the decimal part of a number is less than 1 or greater than or equal to 10, use the power rules to rewrite the number in scientific notation.

3. Write in scientific notation.

a) 132.4×10^3

$= (1.324 \times 10^2) \times 10^3$

$= 1.324 \times 10^5$

b) 0.075×10^5

c) 56.7×10^{-4}

d) 0.0034×10^{-2}

e) 0.0185×10^{-1}

f) 0.874×10^2

4. Multiply, then write the answer in scientific notation.

a) $(5.0 \times 10^4) \times 3.1$

$= 15.5 \times 10^4$

$= (1.55 \times 10^1) \times 10^4$

$= 1.55 \times 10^5$

b) $(3.0 \times 10^{-4}) \times 4.3$

c) $(9.1 \times 10^8) \times 7.0$

d) $(4.0 \times 10^4) \times 2.1$

e) $(6.0 \times 10^{-2}) \times 2.5$

f) $(8.3 \times 10) \times 3.0$

5. Divide, then write the answer in scientific notation.

a) $(0.4 \times 10^6) \div 5.0$

$= 0.08 \times 10^6$

$= (8.0 \times 10^{-2}) \times 10^6$

$= 8.0 \times 10^4$

b) $(3.6 \times 10^{-2}) \div 4.0$

c) $(4.2 \times 10^{-4}) \div 6.0$

d) $(0.06 \times 10^{-2}) \div 2.0$

e) $(0.09 \times 10^8) \div 3.0$

f) $(0.42 \times 10^{-4}) \div 7.0$

To multiply a number in scientific notation by a power of 10, use the power rules to find the product of the powers.

Example: $(2.6 \times 10^3) \times 10^4$

$= 2.6 \times (10^3 \times 10^4)$

$= 2.6 \times 10^7$

6. Multiply.

a) $(3.4 \times 10^5) \times 10^3$

$= 3.4 \times (10^5 \times 10^3)$

$= 3.4 \times 10^8$

b) $(8.12 \times 10^{-4}) \times 10^7$

c) $10^{-2} \times (4.28 \times 10^{-3})$

d) $(9.8 \times 10^{-4}) \times 10^{-3}$

e) $(2.04 \times 10^{-2}) \times 10^6$

f) $10^3 \times (5.78 \times 10^7)$

7. The Earth takes one year to travel around the Sun. It travels approximately 9.4×10^8 km during one orbit. Approximately how many kilometers does it travel in 5 years? Write your answer in scientific notation.

8. Five grains of rice have a mass of 1.4×10^{-4} kg. Find the mass in grams of one grain of rice. Write your answer in scientific notation.

9. A virus cell used in an experiment has a mass of 1.5×10^{-15} g. What is the mass of 300 virus cells? Write your answer in scientific notation.

10. A grain of sand has a mass of approximately 2.4×10^{-3} g. There are approximately 10^9 grains of sand in a cubic meter of sand. Find the approximate mass in grams of a cubic meter of sand. Write your answer in scientific notation.

11. There are approximately 10^9 people in China. If the average weight per person is approximately 6.0×10^4 g, what is the approximate weight in grams of all the people in China? Write your answer in scientific notation.

20. More Operations with Scientific Notation

To multiply two numbers in scientific notation:	Example: $(4.0 \times 10^3) \times (3.0 \times 10^5)$
Step 1: Multiply the decimals and multiply the powers.	$= (4.0 \times 3.0) \times (10^3 \times 10^5)$
	$= 12 \times 10^8$

1. Multiply the decimals and multiply the powers.

   a) $(5.0 \times 10^{-2}) \times (7.0 \times 10^4)$ b) $(4.0 \times 10^2) \times (3.0 \times 10^5)$ c) $(7.0 \times 10^{-4}) \times (6.0 \times 10^{-3})$

Step 2: If the decimal part of a number is not in the correct range, rewrite it using scientific notation and use the power rule to multiply powers with the same base.	Example: 12×10^8
	$= (1.2 \times 10^1) \times 10^8$
	$= 1.2 \times 10^9$

2. Write the number in scientific notation.

   a) 283.4×10^3 b) 0.375×10^4 c) 623.7×10^{-3}

3. Multiply the numbers and write the answer in scientific notation.

   a) $(7.2 \times 10^4) \times (2.0 \times 10^3)$ b) $(2.3 \times 10^{-2}) \times (5.0 \times 10^6)$ c) $(4.2 \times 10^{-2}) \times (3.0 \times 10^{-3})$

   $= 14.4 \times 10^7$

   $= (1.44 \times 10^1) \times 10^7$

   $= 1.44 \times 10^8$

To divide two numbers in scientific notation:	Example: $\dfrac{2.8 \times 10^5}{4.0 \times 10^2} = \dfrac{2.8}{4.0} \times \dfrac{10^5}{10^2}$
Step 1: Divide the decimals and divide the powers.	$= 0.7 \times 10^3$

4. Divide the decimals and divide the powers.

   a) $\dfrac{9.6 \times 10^6}{3.0 \times 10^4}$ b) $\dfrac{3.6 \times 10^4}{9.0 \times 10^7}$ c) $\dfrac{8.4 \times 10^4}{4.0 \times 10^{-1}}$

5. Divide, then write the answer in scientific notation.

a) $\dfrac{4.2 \times 10^4}{7.0 \times 10^7}$

$= 0.6 \times 10^{-3}$

$= (6.0 \times 10^{-1}) \times 10^{-3}$

$= 6.0 \times 10^{-4}$

b) $\dfrac{2.8 \times 10^8}{4.0 \times 10^4}$

c) $\dfrac{4.5 \times 10^7}{9.0 \times 10^2}$

6. A dripping faucet leaks 5.0×10^{-4} L of water every second. There are approximately 3.2×10^7 seconds in a year. Approximately how many liters of water does the faucet leak in a year? Write your answer in scientific notation.

7. In 2012, approximately 2.6×10^9 cases of bottled water were sold in the United States. There are 6.0×10^3 mL of water in a case. Approximately how many milliliters of bottled water were sold that year? Write your answer in scientific notation.

8. In 2013, the population of the United States was approximately 3.2×10^8. The total cost of health care in 2013 was approximately $\$2.88 \times 10^{12}$. What was the approximate cost of health care per person? Write your answer in decimal form.

9. In 2013, the population of India was approximately 1.25×10^9. The population of South Korea was approximately 5.0×10^7. Approximately how many times as many people lived in India as lived in South Korea in 2013? Write your answer in decimal form.

10. In 2013, the population of the United States was approximately 3.2×10^8.

a) If a typical family household has 4 people, how many households were there? Write your answer in scientific notation.

b) The typical family household wastes approximately $2,200 in food each year. What is the approximate value of the food wasted each year by the entire country? Write your answer in decimal form.

21. Estimating Using Scientific Notation (Advanced)

1. Round the decimal part of the number to the nearest whole number.

   a) $2.7 \times 10^3 \approx 3 \times 10^3$

   b) $8.1 \times 10^{-2} \approx$

   c) $4.3 \times 10^{-1} \approx$

   d) $5.79 \times 10^8 \approx$

   e) $6.03 \times 10^{-5} \approx$

   f) $9.86 \times 10^7 \approx$

To estimate a product of numbers written in scientific notation:

Step 1: Round the decimal part of each number.

Step 2: Multiply the whole numbers and multiply the powers.

Example: $(4.23 \times 10^{-5}) \times (2.99 \times 10^2)$

$\approx (4 \times 10^{-5}) \times (3 \times 10^2)$

$= 12 \times 10^{-3}$

---

2. Round the decimal part of each number, then multiply to estimate.

   a) $(3.17 \times 10^{-4}) \times (5.69 \times 10^3)$ b) $(7.89 \times 10^2) \times (2.14 \times 10^{-3})$ c) $(6.8 \times 10^9) \times (3.29 \times 10^{-5})$

Step 3: If the decimal part of an answer is not in the right range, rewrite the answer using scientific notation.

Example: 12×10^{-3}

$= (1.2 \times 10^1) \times 10^{-3}$

$= 1.2 \times 10^{-2}$

---

3. Estimate the product. Write the answer in scientific notation.

   a) $(5.9 \times 10^3) \times (4.12 \times 10^5)$ b) $(2.9 \times 10^{-2}) \times (6.89 \times 10^3)$ c) $(5.14 \times 10^{-3}) \times (9.7 \times 10^{-5})$

   $\approx (6 \times 10^3) \times (4 \times 10^5)$

   $= 24 \times 10^8$

   $= (2.4 \times 10^1) \times 10^8$

   $= 2.4 \times 10^9$

To estimate a quotient of numbers written in scientific notation:

Step 1: Round the decimal part of each number.

Step 2: Divide the whole numbers and divide the powers.

Example: $\dfrac{3.89 \times 10^7}{8.1 \times 10^2} \approx \dfrac{4}{8} \times \dfrac{10^7}{10^2}$

$= 0.5 \times 10^5$

---

4. Round the decimal part of each scientific notation, then divide.

   a) $\dfrac{1.99 \times 10^5}{5.2 \times 10^3}$

   b) $\dfrac{7.8 \times 10^{-1}}{2.1 \times 10^2}$

   c) $\dfrac{5.7 \times 10^3}{7.92 \times 10^{-2}}$

Step 3: If the decimal part of the answer is not in the right range, rewrite the answer using scientific notation.

Example: 0.5×10^5
$$= (5.0 \times 10^{-1}) \times 10^5$$
$$= 5.0 \times 10^4$$

5. Estimate the quotient. Write the answer in scientific notation.

a) $\dfrac{3.94 \times 10^3}{4.8 \times 10^5}$

$\approx \dfrac{4}{5} \times \dfrac{10^3}{10^5}$

$= 0.8 \times 10^{-2}$

$= (8.0 \times 10^{-1}) \times 10^{-2}$

$= 8.0 \times 10^{-3}$

b) $\dfrac{2.75 \times 10^2}{5.89 \times 10^{-1}}$

c) $\dfrac{1.9 \times 10^3}{7.9 \times 10^{-4}}$

6. Estimate by first changing each number into scientific notation.

a) $3{,}276{,}745{,}892 \times 0.00592$

$\approx (3.0 \times 10^9) \times (6.0 \times 10^{-3})$

$= 18 \times 10^6 = 1.8 \times 10^7$

b) $\dfrac{83{,}237}{0.0195}$

$\approx \dfrac{8.0 \times 10^4}{2.0 \times 10^{-2}} =$

c) $0.00584 \times 712{,}568$

d) $\dfrac{0.0019}{5{,}387}$

7. 12.01 g of carbon has approximately 602,214,129,000,000,000,000,000 atoms. What is the approximate mass of one atom of carbon?

8. One cubic kilometer of water contains 10^{12} liters of water. Each liter of water has approximately 3.3×10^{25} water molecules. There are approximately 1.4×10^9 cubic kilometers of water on Earth. Find the approximate number of water molecules on the planet.

9. The speed of light is approximately 3.0×10^8 meters per second. There are 31,536,000 seconds in a year. The Antlia Dwarf galaxy is approximately 4.04×10^{22} meters away from Earth. If an astronaut could travel at the speed of light, approximately how many years would it take the astronaut to reach Antlia Dwarf?

22. Power of a Power

1. Write the power as a product.

a) $3^4 =$

b) $7^6 =$

c) $9^4 =$

2. Complete the table.

Base	Exponent	Power	Product
2	5	2^5	$2 \times 2 \times 2 \times 2 \times 2$
3	4		
			$4 \times 4 \times 4$
		8^3	
5			1

The base of a power can also be a power. This is called a **power of a power**.

$\left(2^3\right)^4$

power

base $= 2^3$

exponent $= 4$

$\left(2^3\right)^4 = 2^3 \times 2^3 \times 2^3 \times 2^3$

multiply 2^3 four times

3. Write the base and exponent for the power of a power.

a) $\left(3^2\right)^5$ base = _____

   exponent = _____

b) $\left(7^4\right)^3$ base = _____

   exponent = _____

c) $\left(9^8\right)^0$ base = _____

   exponent = _____

4. Write as a product of powers.

a) $\left(2^6\right)^4$

   $= 2^6 \times 2^6 \times 2^6 \times 2^6$

b) $\left(4^5\right)^3$

c) $\left(9^2\right)^5$

5. Write as a power of a power.

a) $3^4 \times 3^4 \times 3^4 \times 3^4 \times 3^4$

   $= \left(3^4\right)^5$

b) $9^2 \times 9^2 \times 9^2$

c) $2^4 \times 2^4 \times 2^4 \times 2^4 \times 2^4 \times 2^4$

> REMINDER: To multiply powers with the same base, keep the base and add the exponents.
>
> Examples: $2^3 \times 2^5$
> $= 2^{3+5}$
> $= 2^8$
>
> $10^4 \times 10^2 \times 10^3$
> $= 10^{4+2+3}$
> $= 10^9$

6. Write the power of a power as a product of powers. Then multiply powers with the same base.

a) $\left(2^4\right)^3$

$= 2^4 \times 2^4 \times 2^4$

$= 2^{4+4+4}$

$= 2^{12}$

b) $\left(6^5\right)^4$

c) $\left(7^2\right)^5$

d) $\left(9^4\right)^2$

e) $\left(5^3\right)^3$

f) $\left(8^1\right)^5$

7. In Question 6, what do you notice about the original exponents and the exponent in the final answer?

_____

> To find the power of a power, keep the base and multiply the exponents.
>
> Examples: $\left(2^4\right)^3 = 2^{4 \times 3} = 2^{12}$ $\left(4^6\right)^5 = 4^{6 \times 5} = 4^{30}$

8. Write the power of a power as a single power.

a) $\left(7^5\right)^2 = 7^{5 \times 2}$

$= 7^{10}$

b) $\left(3^8\right)^5$

c) $\left(10^4\right)^7$

d) $\left(8^9\right)^7$

e) $\left(9^6\right)^5$

f) $\left(2^{13}\right)^1$

9. Grace thinks that $5^4 \times 5^3$ and $\left(5^4\right)^3$ are the same. To see if she is correct, write each expression as a product then as a single power. Are they the same? Explain.

_____

_____

23. Power of a Product or Quotient

The base of a power can also be a product. This is called a **power of a product**.

$$(2 \times 3)^4 = (2 \times 3) \times (2 \times 3) \times (2 \times 3) \times (2 \times 3)$$

↑ power of a product

multiply 2×3 four times

1. Write as a product.

   a) $(2 \times 4)^3$

   $= (2 \times 4) \times (2 \times 4) \times (2 \times 4)$

   b) $(4 \times 9)^2$

   c) $(6 \times 8)^4$

2. Write as a power of a product.

   a) $(5 \times 6) \times (5 \times 6) \times (5 \times 6)$

   $= (5 \times 6)^3$

   b) $(9 \times 3) \times (9 \times 3)$

   c) $(4 \times 2) \times (4 \times 2) \times (4 \times 2) \times (4 \times 2)$

The associative property of multiplication lets us change the order of the numbers being multiplied.

Example: $(2 \times 4)^3 = (2 \times 4) \times (2 \times 4) \times (2 \times 4)$

$= (2 \times 2 \times 2) \times (4 \times 4 \times 4)$

$= 2^3 \times 4^3$

3. Write as a product. Then use the associative property to write as a product of powers.

   a) $(7 \times 2)^3$

   $= (7 \times 2) \times (7 \times 2) \times (7 \times 2)$

   $= (7 \times 7 \times 7) \times (2 \times 2 \times 2)$

   $= 7^3 \times 2^3$

   b) $(9 \times 8)^2$

   c) $(5 \times 6)^4$

4. In Question 3, what do you notice about the base and exponents in the original question and the final answer?

_____

To evaluate the power of a product, apply the exponent separately to each factor, and then multiply.

Example: $(3 \times 5)^4 = 3^4 \times 5^4$

5. Write the power of a product as a product of powers.

   a) $(4 \times 5)^3 = 4^3 \times 5^3$

   b) $(8 \times 2)^9 =$

   c) $(6 \times 12)^7 =$

   d) $(7 \times 9)^5 =$

   e) $(7 \times 3)^4 =$

   Bonus ▶ $(25 \times 8)^{100} =$

6. Write the product of powers as a power of a product.

   a) $7^2 \times 8^2 = (7 \times 8)^2$

   b) $4^6 \times 5^6 =$

   c) $7^4 \times 8^4 =$

   d) $3^9 \times 6^9 =$

   e) $8^4 \times 9^4 =$

   Bonus ▶ $8^{927} \times 3^{927} =$

The base of a power can also be a quotient. This is called a **power of a quotient**.

Example:

$$\left(\frac{2}{3}\right)^4 = \left(\frac{2}{3}\right) \times \left(\frac{2}{3}\right) \times \left(\frac{2}{3}\right) \times \left(\frac{2}{3}\right)$$

7. Write as a product.

a) $\left(\frac{3}{4}\right)^3 = \left(\frac{3}{4}\right) \times \left(\frac{3}{4}\right) \times \left(\frac{3}{4}\right)$

b) $\left(\frac{5}{3}\right)^2 =$

c) $\left(\frac{4}{5}\right)^3 =$

8. Write as a power of a quotient.

a) $\left(\frac{5}{7}\right) \times \left(\frac{5}{7}\right) \times \left(\frac{5}{7}\right) \times \left(\frac{5}{7}\right) = \left(\frac{5}{7}\right)^4$

b) $\left(\frac{7}{8}\right) \times \left(\frac{7}{8}\right) \times \left(\frac{7}{8}\right) \times \left(\frac{7}{8}\right) =$

c) $\left(\frac{9}{4}\right) \times \left(\frac{9}{4}\right) =$

We can multiply the numerators and denominators to write the power of a quotient as a quotient of powers.

Example:

$$\left(\frac{4}{5}\right)^3 = \left(\frac{4}{5}\right) \times \left(\frac{4}{5}\right) \times \left(\frac{4}{5}\right) = \frac{4 \times 4 \times 4}{5 \times 5 \times 5} = \frac{4^3}{5^3}$$

9. Write as a product of quotients, then as a quotient of powers.

a) $\left(\frac{5}{4}\right)^3 = \left(\frac{5}{4}\right) \times \left(\frac{5}{4}\right) \times \left(\frac{5}{4}\right)$

$= \frac{5 \times 5 \times 5}{4 \times 4 \times 4}$

$= \frac{5^3}{4^3}$

b) $\left(\frac{9}{2}\right)^3$

c) $\left(\frac{5}{8}\right)^2$

10. In Question 9, what do you notice about the base and exponents in the original question and the final answer?

_____

To evaluate the power of a quotient, apply the exponent to the numerator and to the denominator.

Example:

$$\left(\frac{2}{3}\right)^4 = \frac{2^4}{3^4}$$

11. Write the power of a quotient as a quotient of powers.

a) $\left(\frac{3}{5}\right)^4 = \frac{3^4}{5^4}$

b) $\left(\frac{5}{7}\right)^6 =$

c) $\left(\frac{7}{3}\right)^5 =$

d) $\left(\frac{8}{3}\right)^9 =$

e) $\left(\frac{7}{3}\right)^2 =$

Bonus ▶ $\left(\frac{2}{7}\right)^{453} =$

24. Summary of Exponent Rules

REMINDER:	Power Rule	Example
	To multiply powers with the same base, keep the base and add the exponents.	$2^5 \times 2^4 = 2^9$
	To divide powers with the same base, keep the base and subtract the exponents.	$2^7 \div 2^3 = 2^4$
	A power with exponent zero is equal to 1.	$2^0 = 1$
	A power with a negative exponent is equal to a unit fraction with a positive exponent in the denominator.	$2^{-3} = \dfrac{1}{2^3}$
	To rewrite the power of a power, keep the base and multiply the exponents.	$\left(2^3\right)^4 = 2^{12}$
	To rewrite the power of a product, apply the exponent to each factor.	$(2 \times 3)^4 = 2^4 \times 3^4$
	To rewrite the power of a quotient, apply the exponent to the numerator and the denominator.	$\left(\dfrac{2}{3}\right)^4 = \dfrac{2^4}{3^4}$

1. Circle the expression if it is a product of powers. Underline it if it is a power of a product. Double underline it if it is a power of a power.

   a) $\left(2^3\right)^4$ b) $2^3 \times 2^4$ c) $(2 \times 3)^4$ d) $4^3 \times 4^5$ e) $\left(4 \times 3\right)^5$

   f) $5^6 \times 5^7$ g) $\left(5^6\right)^7$ h) $(5 \times 6)^7$ i) $(9 \times 2)^3$ j) $\left(9^3\right)^2$

2. Circle the expression if it is a power of a quotient. Underline the expression if it is a quotient of powers.

   a) $\dfrac{5^6}{5^2}$ b) $\left(\dfrac{5}{2}\right)^3$ c) $\left(\dfrac{3}{8}\right)^4$ d) $\left(\dfrac{4}{3}\right)^8$ e) $\dfrac{3^2}{3^8}$

3. Find the power rule that applies and use the rule to find an equivalent expression.

   a) $10^2 \times 10^5$ b) $\dfrac{8^6}{8^4}$ c) $\left(\dfrac{5}{2}\right)^4$ d) 5^0 e) 3^{-2}

   $= 10^7$

   f) $(7 \times 3)^4$ g) $8^2 \times 8^7$ h) 23^0 i) $\left(4^2\right)^3$ j) $2^7 \div 2^4$

4. Carlos says that $2^3 + 2^4 = 2^7$. Use your calculator to show he is incorrect. Explain why Carlos cannot keep the base and add the exponents in this example.

5. Write the expression as a power with a single base. More than one power rule may be required.

a) $(2^6 \times 2^3) \div 2^4$

$= 2^{6+3} \div 2^4$

$= 2^{9-4}$

$= 2^5$

b) $(3^4)^2 \times 3^5$

c) $(5^6 \times 5^3) \div (5^2 \times 5^4)$

d) $(2^5)^3 \div (2^3)^4$

e) $\dfrac{(-3)^2(-3)^8}{((-3)^2)^3}$

f) $\left(\dfrac{3}{4}\right)^2 \times \left(\dfrac{3}{4}\right)^5 \div \left(\left(\dfrac{3}{4}\right)^2\right)^3$

6. Evaluate using the power rules and the correct order of operations.

a) $2^3 \times 2^4 - (2^3)^2$

$= 2^7 - 2^6$

$= 128 - 64$

$= 64$

b) $3^7 \div 3^4 + 3^0$

c) $\left(\dfrac{2}{3}\right)^2 - \left(\dfrac{1}{3}\right)^2$

d) $2^{-4} - \left(\dfrac{1}{4}\right)^2$

e) $(8 - 6)^{-3}$

f) $(0.2)^3 - 8 \times 10^{-3}$

7. Write the number as a power of 2.

a) $16 = 2^{\square}$

b) $4 = 2^{\square}$

c) $8 = 2^{\square}$

8. Write as a power of 2 by changing the base and using the power of a power rule.

a) 16^3

$= (2^4)^3$

$= 2^{4 \times 3}$

$= 2^{12}$

b) 4^7

c) 8^5

9. Write the number as a power of 3.

a) $81 = 3^{\square}$

b) $27 = 3^{\square}$

c) $9 = 3^{\square}$

10. Write as a power of 3 by changing the base and then using the power of a power rule.

a) 81^2

$= (3^4)^2$

$= 3^{4 \times 2}$

$= 3^8$

b) 27^5

c) 9^8

11. Write the fraction as a power of 2 with a negative exponent.

a) $\dfrac{1}{2^3} = 2^{\boxed{}}$

b) $\dfrac{1}{2^5} = 2^{\boxed{}}$

c) $\dfrac{1}{2^4} = 2^{\boxed{}}$

12. Write the denominator as a power of 2. Then write the fraction as a power of 2 with a negative exponent.

a) $\dfrac{1}{8}$

$= \dfrac{1}{2^3}$

$= 2^{-3}$

b) $\dfrac{1}{32}$

c) $\dfrac{1}{16}$

13. Write the fraction as a power of 2 by changing the base and then using the power of a power rule.

a) $\left(\dfrac{1}{16}\right)^3$

$= \left(\dfrac{1}{2^4}\right)^3$

$= \left(2^{-4}\right)^3$

$= 2^{-4 \times 3}$

$= 2^{-12}$

b) $\left(\dfrac{1}{8}\right)^2$

c) $\left(\dfrac{1}{32}\right)^{-3}$

14. Write the fraction as a power of 3 with a negative exponent.

a) $\dfrac{1}{3^4} = 3^{\boxed{}}$

b) $\dfrac{1}{3^2} = 3^{\boxed{}}$

c) $\dfrac{1}{3^3} = 3^{\boxed{}}$

15. Write the denominator as a power of 3. Then write the fraction as a power of 3 with a negative exponent.

a) $\dfrac{1}{81}$

$= \dfrac{1}{3^4}$

$= 3^{-4}$

b) $\dfrac{1}{9}$

c) $\dfrac{1}{27}$

16. Write the fraction as a power of 3 by changing the base and then using the power of a power rule.

a) $\left(\dfrac{1}{9}\right)^4$

b) $\left(\dfrac{1}{27}\right)^4$

c) $\left(\dfrac{1}{81}\right)^{-2}$

25. Variables and Expressions

1. Look at the picture on the right. Write an expression for the cost of renting the boat for ...

Boat rental
$8 an hour

  a) 2 hours: $\underline{\quad 8 \times 2 \quad}$ b) 5 hours: $\underline{\qquad}$ c) 6 hours: $\underline{\qquad}$

A **variable** is a letter or symbol that represents a number (for example, x, n, or H).

An **algebraic expression** is a combination of one or more variables, operation signs, numbers, and sometimes brackets.

Examples: $x + 1$ $3 + 4 \times T$ $4.25 + (-3 - t) \times h$

---

2. Write an expression for the distance a car would travel at the given speed and in the given time.

  a) Speed: 40 mi per hour   b) Speed: 60 mi per hour   c) Speed: 60 mi per hour
     Time: 2 hours   Time: 3 hours   Time: h hours

   Distance: $\underline{\;40 \times 2\;}$ mi   Distance: $\underline{\qquad}$ mi   Distance: $\underline{\qquad}$ mi

---

In the product of a number and a variable, the multiplication sign is usually dropped.

Examples: $2 \times N$ can be written as $2N$ and $7 \times a$ can be written as $7a$

---

3. Look at the picture on the right. Write an algebraic expression for the cost of renting skis for ...

  a) h hours: $\underline{\;6 \times h\;}$ or $\underline{\;6h\;}$ b) n hours: $\underline{\qquad}$ or $\underline{\qquad}$

  c) t hours: $\underline{\qquad}$ or $\underline{\qquad}$ d) x hours: $\underline{\qquad}$ or $\underline{\qquad}$

Ski rental
$6 an hour

When replacing a variable in an expression with a number, we use brackets.

Example: If we replace n with 7, $3n$ is $3(7)$, which is another way to write 3×7.

---

4. Evaluate the expression with $n = 2$.

  a) $5n = 5(2)$ b) $7n = 7(2)$ c) $23n$ d) $30,000n$

      $= 10$ $=$

5. Replace n with 3 and then evaluate.

  a) $4n + 2$ b) $4n - 1$ c) $2n - 5$ d) $2n - 7$

      $= 4(3) + 2$

      $= 12 + 2$

      $= 14$

  e) $3n + 7$ f) $7 + 3n$ g) $11n - 11$ h) $11 \times (n - 1)$

JUMP Math Accumula

6. Replace the variable with the given number and then evaluate.

a) $5h + 2$, $h = 3$

$= 5(3) + 2$

$= 15 + 2$

$= 17$

b) $6n - 4$, $n = 5$

c) $3x - 17$, $x = 7$

d) $12p + 6$, $p = 5$

e) $11 - 3w$, $w = 4$

f) $3 \times (c - 4)$, $c = 6$

In an expression, the **coefficient** of a variable is the number that is multiplied by that variable.

Examples: $5x + 2$ ◄——— the coefficient of x is 5

$w - 7 = 1w - 7$ ◄——— the coefficient of w is 1

$3 - 4x = 3 + (-4x)$ ◄——— the coefficient of x is -4

---

7. Write the coefficient.

a) $3a + 2$ _____

b) $m - 3$ _____

c) $3 - 8w$ _____

d) $2 + 6r$ _____

e) $9 + p$ _____

f) $-5s - 4$ _____

In an expression with two variables, we must name the variables.

Example: $3a - 7b + 5$ ◄——— the coefficient of a is 3

the coefficient of b is -7

---

8. Write the coefficient of x.

a) $3x + 4y + 7$ _____

b) $8x - y + 9$ _____

c) $2u + 4x - 5$ _____

d) $3u - 5x - 8$ _____

e) $9w + 3x + 8y$ _____

f) $-5 + 4w - 3x$ _____

In an expression, a number that is not multiplied by a variable is called a constant term.

Examples: $3x + 4$ ◄——— the constant term is 4

$5x = 5x + 0$ ◄——— the constant term is 0

$7x - 5$ ◄——— the constant term is -5

---

9. Write the constant term.

a) $2x - 4y + 9$ _____

b) $-5x + y + 3$ _____

c) $3u - 4v - 5$ _____

d) $3z + 7p - 4$ _____

e) $7w - x - 4$ _____

Bonus ▶ $2p + 3q - 7r$ _____

---

10. Is -3 the coefficient or the constant term?

a) $3 - 3x$

b) $3x - 3$

c) $-3 - x$

_____

_____

_____

A **flat fee** is a fixed charge that does not depend on how long you rent an item.

Example: A company charges a flat fee of $7 to rent a boat, plus $3 for each hour the boat is used.

11. Write an expression for the cost to rent a boat for …

a) 4 hours
Flat fee: $7
Hourly rate: $5 per hour

$\underline{\quad 4 \times 5 + 7 \quad}$

b) 4 hours
Flat fee: $5
Hourly rate: $6 per hour

$\underline{\qquad\qquad}$

c) 6 hours
Flat fee: $7
Hourly rate: $3 per hour

$\underline{\qquad\qquad}$

d) h hours
Flat fee: $5
Hourly rate: $7

$\underline{\quad 7h + 5 \quad}$

e) t hours
Flat fee: $9
Hourly rate: $5

$\underline{\qquad\qquad}$

f) w hours
Flat fee: $6
Hourly rate: $4

$\underline{\qquad\qquad}$

12. Match the fee for renting a windsurfing board to the correct algebraic expression.

A. $12h + 5$ **B.** $5h + 12$ **C.** $12h$

a) $12 flat fee and $5 for each hour $\underline{\qquad}$

b) $12 for each hour, no flat fee $\underline{\qquad}$

c) $5 flat fee and $12 for each hour $\underline{\qquad}$

13. A taxi ride charges a flat fee of $5 and $2 for every mile traveled. The total is given by the expression $5 + 2m$. Find the cost of taking a taxi for …

a) 4 miles

$5 + 2(4)$

$= 5 + 8$

$= 13$

b) 2 miles

c) 5 miles

14. Gloves cost $4 per pair. The cost of n pairs is $4n$. Anna says that the cost of 3 pairs is $43 and the cost of 5 pairs is $45. What mistake did Anna make?

$\underline{\qquad\qquad\qquad\qquad\qquad\qquad\qquad\qquad\qquad\qquad}$

$\underline{\qquad\qquad\qquad\qquad\qquad\qquad\qquad\qquad\qquad\qquad}$

15. An electrician's fee for an emergency call is a flat fee of $90 plus $20 for every 15 minutes spent on the job.

a) Write an expression to represent the electrician's fee.

b) What would you expect to pay for a 45-minute job?

c) Calculate how long the electrician was at the job if a fee of $170 is charged.

26. Solving Equations Using the Distributive Property

You can rewrite an addition or subtraction expression without brackets and then simplify.

$$7 - 2(3x + 4) = 7 - (6x + 8)$$
$$= 7 - 6x - 8$$
$$= -1 - 6x$$

1. Write the expression without brackets and then simplify.

a) $9x - 3(x + 4)$

$= 9x - (3x + 12)$

$=$

b) $9x - (3x + 4)$

c) $9 - 3(2x + 4)$

d) $9 - 3(2x - 4)$

e) $7 - 2(3 - 8x)$

f) $8x - 3(4 - 5x)$

g) $2 - 4(3 - 2x)$

h) $4x - 3(-7 + 3x)$

i) $(8x + 2) - 4(3 - 2x) + (3x - 5)$

j) $(5 + 4x) + (9 - 4x) - 3(-7 + 3x)$

Bonus ▶ $2(x + 2) + 3(x + 7) - 5(2x - 4)$

2. Ben tries three ways to solve $2(x + 3) = 14$:

Method 1	Method 2	Method 3
$2(x + 3) = 14$	$2(x + 3) = 14$	$2(x + 3) = 14$
$2x + 6 = 14$	$2(x + 3) \div 2 = 14 \div 2$	$2x + 3 = 14$
$2x + 6 - 6 = 14 - 6$	$x + 3 = 7$	$2x + 3 - 3 = 14 - 3$
$2x = 8$	$x + 3 - 3 = 7 - 3$	$2x = 11$
$2x \div 2 = 8 \div 2$	$x = 4$	$2x \div 2 = 11 \div 2$
$x = 4$		$x = \dfrac{11}{2}$

a) Do Ben's three ways give the same answer? _____

b) Substitute $x = 4$ into the expression $2(x + 3)$. Do you get 14? _____

Substitute $x = \dfrac{11}{2}$ into the expression $2(x + 3)$. Do you get 14? _____

What is the correct answer? _____

c) Describe in words each step in Methods 1, 2, and 3. Where did Ben make a mistake in Method 3?

3. Decide whether each solution is correct by substituting the answer into the original expression. For each incorrect solution, describe the mistake. Mark the correct solution with a checkmark.

a)
$$3(x - 1) = 15$$
$$3x - 1 = 15$$
$$3x - 1 + 1 = 15 + 1$$
$$3x = 16$$
$$3x \div 3 = 16 \div 3$$
$$x = \frac{16}{3}$$

$$3(x - 1) = 15$$
$$3x - 3 = 15$$
$$3x - 3 + 3 = 15 + 3$$
$$3x = 18$$
$$3x \div 3 = 18 \div 3$$
$$x = 6$$

b)
$$5(x + 2) = 30$$
$$5(x + 2) \div 5 = 30 \div 5$$
$$x + 2 = 4$$
$$x + 2 - 2 = 4 - 2$$
$$x = 2$$

$$5(x + 2) = 30$$
$$5x + 10 = 30$$
$$5x + 10 - 10 = 30 - 10$$
$$5x = 20$$
$$5x \div 5 = 20 \div 5$$
$$x = 4$$

c)
$$3x + 6 = 21$$
$$3(x + 6) = 21$$
$$x + 6 = 7$$
$$x + 6 - 6 = 7 - 6$$
$$x = 1$$

$$3x + 6 = 21$$
$$3(x + 2) = 21$$
$$x + 2 = 21$$
$$x + 2 - 2 = 21 - 2$$
$$x = 19$$

$$3x + 6 = 21$$
$$3(x + 2) = 21$$
$$x + 2 = 7$$
$$x + 2 - 2 = 7 - 2$$
$$x = 5$$

$$3x + 6 = 21$$
$$3x + 6 - 6 = 21 + 6$$
$$3x = 27$$
$$3x \div 3 = 27 \div 3$$
$$x = 9$$

Remember: an equation is like a set of balanced scales. You can add or subtract the same value on both sides. Example: May solves $8 - x = 3x$ in two steps:

Step 1: She treats x as a number and adds x to both sides.

$$8 - x + x = 3x + x$$
$$8 = 4x$$

Step 2: She divides both sides by 4 to find x.

$$8 \div 4 = 4x \div 4$$
$$2 = x$$

May checks her answer. She replaces x in the equation with 2:　　$8 - 2 = 6$, and $3(2) = 6$ ✓

---

4. Solve the equation. Remember to group like terms.

a)
$$3x = 15 - 2x$$
$$3x + 2x = 15 - 2x + 2x$$
$$5x = 15$$
$$5x \div 5 = 15 \div 5$$
$$x = 3$$

b) $6x = 8 + 4x$

c) $4x - 3x + 4 = 9 - 2x$

d) $4x - 3x + 4 = -6$

e) $5x - 9x + 3 = 4 - (-5)$

f) $3x - 5 - 4x = 17 - 3x - 2$

g) $32 + 2x = 5x + 17$

h) $2x - 4 - 5 = 21 - 13x$

i) $1 - 5x = -6 - 2 - 7 + 4 - x$

In an equation, a term may be moved to the other side of the equal sign, but only if the sign (+ or −) of the term is changed to the opposite sign. Examples:

If	$7 = 5 + 2$	If	$x - 2 = 8$	If	$x + 2 = 5$	If	$2 + 3 = -4 + x$	If	$3x = 15 - 2x$
Then	$7 - 2 = 5$	Then	$x = 8 + 2$	Then	$x = 5 - 2$	Then	$2 + 3 + 4 = x$	Then	$3x + 2x = 15$

5. Move all variable terms to the same side of the equal sign. Hint: a term with x is a variable term.

a) $4x = 2x + 8$

$4x \underline{\ - 2x\ } = 8$

b) $5x = 3x + 6$

$5x \underline{\hspace{2cm}} = 6$

c) $2x = 12 - 4x$

$2x \underline{\hspace{2cm}} = 12$

d) $-2x = 4x - 8$

$-2x \underline{\hspace{2cm}} = -8$

e) $14 - 3x = 4x$

$14 = 4x \underline{\hspace{2cm}}$

f) $7 - 2x = 5x$

$7 = 5x \underline{\hspace{2cm}}$

To solve an equation:

Step 1: If there are brackets, rewrite the equation without them.

Step 2: Move all the variable terms to one side of the equal sign and all the constant terms to the other side.

Step 3: Simplify both sides of the equation.

Step 4: Divide by the coefficient of x.

You just solved for x!

Example:

$3(2x - 3) + 4 = -2(x + 4) - 5$

$6x - 9 + 4 = -2x - 8 - 5$

$6x + 2x = 9 - 4 - 8 - 5$

$8x = -8$

$x = -1$

6. Solve the equation.

a) $-x - 3 = x - 9$

$-3 + 9 = x + x$

$6 = 2x$

$3 = x$

b) $3x - 17 = 5x - 9$

c) $3(x + 5) = x + 7$

d) $3(5 - x) = 2(4 - 5x)$

e) $6 + \dfrac{2}{3}x = 11 - x$

f) $\dfrac{3}{5} + 5x = \dfrac{7}{5} - 3x$

g) $3(x + 4) + 4(5 - x) = 2(x - 2)$

h) $2(3x + 7) = 5(9 - 2x) + 1$

i) $2(3x - 5) + 3(7 - 4x) = 2x + 3$

7. Check your answers to Question 6 by replacing x in the original equation with your answer. Check your answers for parts d) to i) in your notebook.

a) $-3 - 3 = 3 - 9$

$-6 = -6 \checkmark$

b)

c)

27. Advanced Algebra

1. Solve the equation by first moving all variable terms to the same side of the equal sign.

   a) $2x = -3x + 15$

   $2x + 3x = 15$

   $5x = 15$

   $x = 15 \div 5$

   $x = 3$

   b) $5x = 2x + 9$

   c) $8x = 3x + 20$

2. Move all variable terms to one side of the equal sign and all constant terms to the other side.

   a) $-2x + 5 = -4x + 2$

   $-2x + 4x = 2 - 5$

   b) $5x - 3 = 2x + 9$

   c) $2x + 3 = -x + 21$

   d) $-\dfrac{3}{5}x + 5 = \dfrac{1}{5}x + 2$

   $-\dfrac{3}{5}x - \dfrac{1}{5}x = 2 - 5$

   e) $\dfrac{5}{7}x - \dfrac{4}{9} = \dfrac{2}{7}x + \dfrac{1}{9}$

   f) $\dfrac{2}{5} - \dfrac{3}{5}x = \dfrac{1}{5} + \dfrac{2}{5}x$

3. Solve the equation. Hint: Group like terms first, if necessary.

   a) $\dfrac{3}{5}x + 3 = -\dfrac{1}{5}x + 11$

   $\dfrac{3}{5}x + \dfrac{1}{5}x = 11 - 3$

   $\dfrac{4}{5}x = 8$

   $\dfrac{4}{5}x \div \dfrac{4}{5} = 8 \div \dfrac{4}{5} = 8 \times \dfrac{5}{4}$

   $x = 10$

   b) $\dfrac{2}{3}x + 5 = \dfrac{1}{3}x + 6$

   c) $\dfrac{3}{5}x - \dfrac{2}{7} = -\dfrac{2}{5}x + \dfrac{5}{7}$

   d) $\dfrac{5}{9} + 3x = 2x + \dfrac{4}{9}$

   e) $\dfrac{1}{3}(2x - 2) = \dfrac{2}{3}(3 - x)$

   Bonus ▶ $\dfrac{3}{5}(5x - 3) = x - 2$

4. A box contains some red and yellow beads. Let x represent the number of red beads in the box. Write the number of yellow beads in terms of x.

   a) 4 more yellow beads than red beads

   red: ___x___

   yellow: ___$x + 4$___

   b) 3 fewer yellow beads than red beads

   red: _____

   yellow: _____

   c) 5 more red beads than yellow beads

   d) 4 times as many yellow beads as red beads

   e) 2 fewer red beads than yellow beads

   f) 4 times as many red beads as yellow beads

5. A box contains 20 red and yellow beads. Find the numbers of red and yellow beads if ...

a) there are 4 more red beads
    than yellow beads.

    red: ___x___

    yellow: ___x − 4___

    equation: $x +$ ___x − 4___ $= 20$

$$x + x - 4 = 20$$
$$2x = 20 + 4$$
$$2x = 24$$
$$2x \div 2 = 24 \div 2$$
$$x = 12$$

There are 12 red beads and
$12 - 4 = 8$ yellow beads.

b) there are 10 more yellow beads than
    red beads.

c) there are 3 times as many yellow beads
    as red beads.

d) there are 2 more red beads than
    yellow beads.

e) there are 4 times as many red beads
    as yellow beads.

6. Write expressions for the numbers of red, green, and yellow beads in a box.
    Hint: Underline the color that appears in both sentences. Let x represent that color.

a) There are 3 more yellow beads
    than green beads.
    There are 4 times as many
    red beads as green beads

    red: _____

    green: ___x___

    yellow: _____

b) There are 4 fewer yellow beads
    than red beads.
    There are 5 times as many
    green beads as yellow beads

    red: _____

    green: _____

    yellow: _____

c) There are 2 fewer red beads
    than green beads.
    There are 3 more yellow beads
    than green beads.

d) There are 2 more red beads
    than green beads.
    There are 2 times as many
    yellow beads as green beads.

7. There are 5 more red beads than green beads in a box. There are 3 times as many
    yellow beads as red beads. The number of red and green beads is 12 less than the
    number of yellow beads. How many beads are in the box?

8. Liz and Amit went windsurfing together. Liz paid $7 to rent her windsurfing board,
    plus $3 for each hour she surfed. Amit paid $10 for his windsurfing board, plus $2 for
    each hour he surfed. Liz and Amit paid the same amount. How many hours did they
    windsurf together?

9. The boxes have the same perimeter.
    Find the perimeter of each box.

    10

    3x

    5x + 4

    x

28. Applications of Linear Equations

To solve word problems, you turn the words into algebraic expressions. Words such as the following give clues to the operations you need to use:

Add	Subtract	Multiply	Divide
increased by	less than	product	divided by
sum	difference	times	divided into
more than	decreased by	twice as many	
	reduced by		

1. Match each description with the correct algebraic expression.

a) **A.** $4x$ **B.** $x - 2$ **C.** $x + 2$ **D.** $x - 3$ **E.** $x \div 3$ **F.** $3 \div x$

   i)   2 more than a number _____   ii) A number divided by 3 _____

   iii) 2 less than a number _____   iv) 3 divided by a number _____

   v)   A number decreased by 3 _____   vi) The product of a number and 4 _____

b) **A.** $3x$ **B.** $x \div 2$ **C.** $x + 3$ **D.** $x - 4$ **E.** $2x$ **F.** $2 \div x$

   i)   2 divided into a number _____   ii) A number reduced by 4 _____

   iii) 2 divided by a number _____   iv) Twice as many as a number _____

   v)   A number increased by 3 _____   vi) A number times 3 _____

2. Write an algebraic expression for the description.

a) Four more than a number   b) A number decreased by 10   c) The product of 7 and a number

d) A number divided by 8   e) Two less than a number   f) The sum of a number and 7

g) Five times a number   h) Six divided into a number   i) The product of a number and 3

j) Five more than a number,   k) A number reduced by 4,   l) Twice as many as 3 less
   then three times the answer   then multiplied by 2   than a number

---

In word problems, "is" often means "equals" or $=$.
Example: "Two more than a number is seven" can be written $x + 2 = 7$.

---

3. Solve the problem by first writing an equation.

a) Four more than a number is thirty-two.   b) Five less than a number is 19.

c) Five times a number is thirty.   d) A number divided by four is seven.

e) Six divided into a number is four.   f) The product of a number and 5 is forty.

g) A number multiplied by two then   h) A number divided by three then increased
   decreased by five is thirty-five.   by four is seventeen.

i) 3 divided into a number is 2 less than 8.   j) 3 less than a number is 5 times smaller than 20.

k) Three times two more than a number is 17.   l) Three times a number is 14 more than 5.

Two numbers are **consecutive** if one is the next number after the other.

Examples: 6 and 7 are consecutive numbers because 7 is the next number after 6.

6 and 8 are consecutive even numbers because 8 is the next even number after 6.

4. Fill in the blanks.

a) 36, 37, 38, and _____ are consecutive numbers.

b) 4, 6, 8, and _____ are consecutive even numbers.

c) 7 and _____ are consecutive odd numbers.

d) 7 and _____ are consecutive prime numbers.

e) x, $x + 1$, and _____ are consecutive numbers.

f) x is even. x, _____, and _____ are consecutive even numbers.

g) x is odd. x, _____, and _____ are consecutive odd numbers.

5. The sum of three consecutive numbers is 18. What are the numbers?
Solve the problem in two ways.

a) Use a table to list all possible consecutive numbers in order and then find the sums.
Stop when the sum reaches 18.

Three Consecutive Numbers	Their Sum
1, 2, 3	$1 + 2 + 3 = 6$
2, 3, 4	$2 + 3 + 4 = 9$
3, 4, 5	
4, 5, 6	

b) Use algebra.

i) If the smallest of the consecutive numbers is x, write an expression for each of the other numbers.

Smallest number $= x$

Middle number $=$ _____

Largest number $=$ _____

ii) Write an equation to express the statement above: The sum of the three consecutive numbers is 18.

_____ $= 18$

iii) Solve your equation. What is the smallest number? What are the three numbers?

_____

6. The sum of three consecutive even numbers is 42. What are the three numbers?

a) Let the smallest number be x and solve the problem.

b) Let the middle number be x and solve the problem.

c) Let the largest number be x and solve the problem.

d) Did you get the same answer all three ways?

7. a) Answer Question 6 using tables.

b) Did you get the same answer using a table as you did using algebra?

c) Which method do you like better: a table or algebra? Explain.

REMINDER: The area of a rectangle is length multiplied by width, or $A = \ell \times w$ (or $A = \ell w$).

8. a) Evaluate the expression for the area of a rectangle with …

i) $\ell = 2$, $w = 7$

ii) $\ell = 3\frac{1}{5}$, $w = \frac{1}{2}$

iii) $\ell = 3.7$, $w = 10$

b) A rectangle has an area of $5\frac{2}{3}$ and length of $3\frac{1}{2}$. Write an equation for the width w and solve it.

9. a) Write an expression for the perimeter. x stands for the length of one or more unknown sides.

i)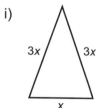

ii)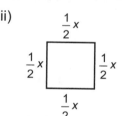

iii)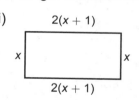

iv)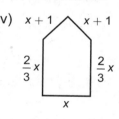

_____   _____   _____   _____

b) The perimeter of each shape in part a) is 28. Find the unknown side lengths.

i)   ii)   iii)   iv)

10. Mark's dad is three times older than Mark. Mark's sister is 2 years younger than Mark. The sum of all three ages is 48. How old is Mark?

Bonus ▶ Randi's sister is half as old as Randi. Randi's mother is $2\frac{1}{2}$ times Randi's age.

Randi's father is 4 years older than Randi's mother. The sum of all four ages is 95. How old was Randi's father when Randi was born?

29. Ratios and Fractions

A fraction compares a part to a whole. A **ratio** can compare a part to a part, or a part to a whole.

Example: ◯ ◯ ☐ ☐ ◯

The **part-to-part ratio** of circles to squares is 3 to 2 or 3 : 2.

The **part-to-whole ratio** of circles to shapes is 3 to 5 or 3 : 5.

1. ☆ ◯ ☐ ◖ ◯ ◯ ☆ ◯ ☐ ◯ ☆ ◯ ◖ ☐ △

   a) The ratio of moons to stars is _____ : _____.   b) The ratio of squares to moons is _____ : _____.

   c) The ratio of stars to circles is _____ : _____.   d) The ratio of triangles to shapes is _____ : _____.

2. a) Write the ratio of vowels (a, e, i, o, u) to consonants (other letters) in the word.

   i) star   _____ : _____   ii) moon   _____ : _____

   iii) oak   _____ : _____   iv) America   _____ : _____

   v) Seattle   _____ : _____   vi) Jefferson _____ : _____

   b) Are the ratios you found in part a) part-to-part ratios or part-to-whole ratios?

   _____

3. Classify the ratio. Circle if it is a part-to-whole ratio. Underline if it is a part-to-part ratio.

   a) vowels in "Maine" : letters in "Maine"   b) vowels in "Oregon" : consonants in "Oregon"

   c) school days in a week to days of the week   d) days in May to days in June

You can think of a part-to-whole ratio as a fraction.

Example: ◯ ◯ △ △ △

The ratio of circles to shapes is 2 to 5 or 2 : 5, so $\frac{2}{5}$ of the shapes are circles.

4. Write a ratio and a fraction.

   a) ◯ ◯ ◯ △ △ △ △   b) ◯ ◯ △ △ △

   circles to shapes = _____ : _____   circles to shapes = _____ : _____

   _____ of the shapes are circles.   _____ of the shapes are circles.

When there are only two parts, you can change a part-to-part ratio to a fraction.

Example: There are 3 circles for every 5 triangles in a set of circles and triangles.

○○○△△△△△

So there are 3 circles for every total of 8 shapes. $\frac{3}{8}$ of the shapes are circles.

5. Write the number of boys (b), girls (g), and students (s) in each class.

a) There are 7 boys and 5 girls in a class. b: __7__ g: __5__ s: __12__

b) There are 11 girls in a class of 20 students. b: _____ g: _____ s: _____

c) There are 6 boys in a class of 11 students. b: _____ g: _____ s: _____

6. Write the fraction of students in the class who are boys and the fraction who are girls.

a) There are 7 boys and 8 girls in the class. b: $\boxed{\dfrac{7}{15}}$ g: $\boxed{}$

b) The ratio of boys to girls in the class is 5 to 6. b: $\boxed{}$ g: $\boxed{}$

c) The ratio of girls to boys in the class is 8 : 7. b: $\boxed{}$ g: $\boxed{}$

7. In Class A, $\frac{2}{5}$ of the students are girls. In Class B, $\frac{5}{8}$ of the students are girls.

a) What is the ratio of girls to boys in each class? A. _____ : _____ B. _____ : _____

b) Which class has more girls than boys? How can you tell from the fraction? How can you tell from the ratio?

In the picture, there are 3 circles for every 2 squares.

There are also 6 circles for every 4 squares.

The ratios 3 : 2 and 6 : 4 are **equivalent ratios** because they both compare circles to squares in the same set.

8. Find two equivalent ratios for the picture.

a)

circles to squares = 1 : _____ = 2 : _____

b)

circles to squares = 2 : _____ = 6 : _____

9. Skip count to write a sequence of three equivalent ratios.

a)   3 : 2   b)   3 : 5   c)   5 : 8   d)   3 : 10

   = __6__ : __4__   = ____ : ____   = ____ : ____   = ____ : ____

   = __9__ : __6__   = ____ : ____   = ____ : ____   = ____ : ____

   = ____ : ____   = ____ : ____   = ____ : ____   = ____ : ____

There are 5 girls for every 2 boys in the class.
There are 20 girls in the class.

To find out how many boys are in the class,
write a sequence of equivalent ratios.

Stop when there are 20 girls. ——————————————➔

Girls		Boys
5	:	2
10	:	4
15	:	6
20	:	8

◀—— There are 8 boys in the class.

---

10. Write a sequence of equivalent ratios to solve the problem.

a) There are 5 boys for every 4 girls in a class
with 20 boys. How many girls are in the class?

Boys   Girls

b) There are 7 red beads for every 3 blue beads
in a bracelet. The bracelet has 21 red beads.
How many blue beads are there?

Red   Blue

c) A recipe for soup calls for 2 cups of carrots
for every 1 cup of lentils. How many cups of
carrots are needed for 5 cups of lentils?

Carrots   Lentils

d) A car travels 100 km on 6 L of gas. The tank
holds 36 L. How many kilometers can the
car travel on a full tank of gas?

Distance (km)   Gas (L)

e) To make liquid plant food, you mix 3 ounces of fertilizer with 2 gallons of water.
How much water do you need for 12 ounces of fertilizer?

           JUMP Math Accumula

There are 3 boys for every 2 girls in a class of 20 students.

To find out how many boys are in the class, write a sequence of equivalent ratios.

Stop when the parts add to 20.

12 boys + 8 girls = 20 students, so there are 12 boys in the class.

Boys		Girls	Total
3	:	2	5
6	:	4	10
9	:	6	15
12	:	8	20

11. Write a sequence of equivalent ratios to solve the problem.

a) There are 5 boys for every 6 girls in a class of 33 students. How many girls are in the class?

    Boys   Girls   Total

b) A recipe for lentil stew calls for 1 cup of lentils for 3 cups of rice. How much rice do you need for 12 cups of lentil stew?

    Lentils   Rice   Total

c) A chain of music stores knows that for every 97 good keyboards received, there will be 3 defective ones. How many defective keyboards are in a shipment of 500 keyboards?

    Good   Defective   Total

d) 28 people voted in an election with 2 candidates. There were 2 votes for Helen for every 5 votes for Will. How many people voted for Will?

    Helen   Will   Total

e) A company spends $7,000 on TV advertising for every $4,000 spent on radio advertising. The company budget for TV and radio advertising is $77,000. How much of the budget is spent on each type of advertising?

12. In Class A, the ratio of boys to girls is 3 : 4. There are 35 students in total. In Class B, $\frac{5}{9}$ of the students are girls. There are 36 students in total. Which class has more boys?

30. Ratio Tables

The numbers in a ratio are called **terms**. To create an equivalent ratio, multiply each term in the ratio by the same number.

Example: There are 2 circles and 1 square. Draw them four times.

Multiply each term by 4.

So the ratio of circles to squares is:

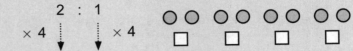

$$\times 4 \downarrow \quad \downarrow \times 4$$
$$8 : 4$$

1. What number are both terms multiplied by to make the second ratio?

   a)　　1 : 3
   ×_4_ ↓ ↓ ×___
   　　4 : 12

   b)　　2 : 7
   ×___ ↓ ↓ ×___
   　　6 : 21

   c)　　5 : 3
   ×___ ↓ ↓ ×___
   　　25 : 15

   d)　　3 : 2
   ×___ ↓ ↓ ×___
   　　30 : 20

2. Multiply both terms by the same number to make an equivalent ratio.

   a)　　1 : 4
   × 3 ↓ ↓ × 3
   ___ : ___

   b)　　5 : 7
   × 5 ↓ ↓ × 5
   ___ : ___

   c)　　5 : 3
   × 10 ↓ ↓ × 10
   ___ : ___

   d)　　8 : 2
   × 2 ↓ ↓ × 2
   ___ : ___

3. What is the first term multiplied by? Multiply the second term by the same number.

   a)　　2 : 3
   ×_5_ ↓ ↓ ×_5_
   　　10 : _15_

   b)　　7 : 3
   ×___ ↓ ↓ ×___
   　　28 : ___

   c)　　11 : 12
   ×___ ↓ ↓ ×___
   　　77 : ___

   d)　　4 : 10
   ×___ ↓ ↓ ×___
   　　48 : ___

A **ratio table** has equivalent ratios in every row. To make a ratio table, make a list of equivalent ratios.

You can find each row from the first row by multiplying both terms in the ratio by the same number.

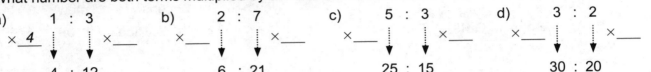

First Term	Second Term
3	5
6	10
9	15
12	20

4. Multiply to complete the ratio table.

   a) 5 : 1　　　b) 2 : 5　　　c) 7 : 3

	a)		b)		c)	
First row	5	1	2	5	7	3
First row × 2	10	2				
First row × 3	15	3				
First row × 4	20	4				

5. Complete a ratio table for the ratio. Multiply the first row by 2 and then by 3.

a)   3 : 2

3	2
6	4
9	6

×2
×3

b)   1 : 5

1	5

c)   6 : 5

6	5

d)   4 : 7

4	7

6. Find the missing number(s) in the ratio table.

a)   3 : 7

3	7
6	14
9	

b)   5 : 2

5	2
10	
	6

c)   1 : 10

1	10
	20
3	

d)   6 : ____

6	
12	20
18	

Sometimes a ratio table has only two rows. The rows show equivalent ratios.

---

7. What number do you multiply the first row by to get the second row? Find the missing number in the ratio table.

a) × _2_

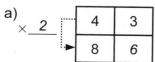

4	3
8	6

b) × ____

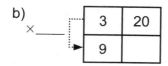

3	20
9	

c) × ____

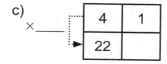

4	1
22	

d)

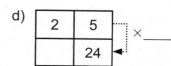

2	5
	24

× ____

8. Solve the problem by making a ratio table.

a) Five bus tickets cost $13. How much will 20 tickets cost?

Tickets	Cost ($)
5	13

b) A box can hold 20 lb. How many boxes are needed to ship 100 lb of goods?

Boxes	Weight (lb)
1	20

c) Mike earns $155 in 2 weeks. How much money will he earn in 8 weeks?

Weeks	Earnings ($)

d) A 10 ft long wall is made of 525 bricks. How many bricks are needed for a wall 50 ft long?

Length (ft)	Bricks

Bonus ▶ A car uses 3.1 gal of fuel for 100 miles. The fuel tank can hold 12.4 gal of fuel. How far can you drive the car if the tank is half full?

31. Graphing Ratios

We use a pair of numbers in brackets to give the position of a point on a coordinate grid. The numbers are called **coordinates** of the point.

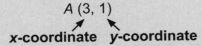

A (3, 1)
x-coordinate   **y-coordinate**

B (1, 3)
x-coordinate   **y-coordinate**

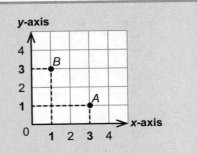

The *x*-coordinate is always written first. The pair of numbers is also called an **ordered pair**.

1. Find the coordinates of the points.

A (__1__ , __3__)   B (_____ , _____)

C (_____ , _____)   D (_____ , _____)

E (_____ , _____)   F (_____ , _____)

G (_____ , _____)   H (_____ , _____)

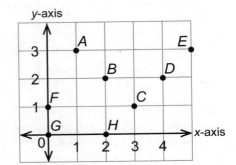

We use number lines to mark the grid lines.

The number lines are called **axes**. One number line is called an **axis**.

The axes meet at the point (0, 0), called the **origin**.

Axes can have positive and negative numbers, fractions, and decimals. You can label axes using skip counting.

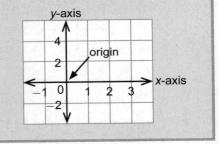

2. Plot and label the points on the coordinate grid. After you plot a point, cross out the coordinates.

a) $A\left(2.5, 3\frac{1}{4}\right)$ $B\,(3, 2)$ $C\,(3.5, 1)$

   $D\left(1, 1\frac{3}{4}\right)$ $E\left(1\frac{1}{2}, 0\right)$ $F\left(0, \frac{1}{2}\right)$

b) $A\,(3, -1)$ $B\,(2, 2)$ $C\,(4, 1)$

   $D\,(1, -2)$ $E\,(1, 0)$ $F\,(2, -3)$

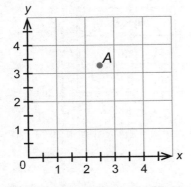

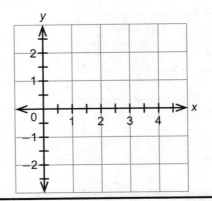

3. a) All the coordinates are whole numbers. Write the coordinates of the points.

i)
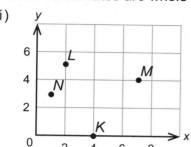

ii)
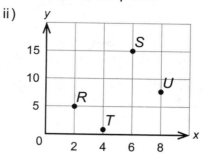

K (_____, _____), L (_____, _____),

M (_____, _____), N (_____, _____)

R (_____, _____), S (_____, _____),

T (_____, _____), U (_____, _____)

b) Plot the points on the grid above. Cross out the coordinates as you go.

i) *O* (5, 6), *P* (0, 7), *Q* (9, 1)

ii) *V* (0, 12), *W* (5, 0), **Bonus** ▶ *Z* (1.5, 14)

4. a) Make a ratio table for the ratio. Write an ordered pair for each row of the table.

i) 1 : 2

1	2	*(1, 2)*
2	4	*(2, 4)*
3	6	*(3, 6)*
4	8	*(4, 8)*

ii) 1 : 1

1	1	

iii) 2 : 3

2	3	

b) Plot the ordered pairs from part a) on the grid and connect the points.

i)

ii)
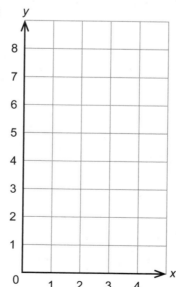

iii)
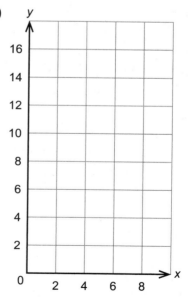

c) Extend the line to intersect the axes. What do you notice about the intersection points?

To graph a ratio:

Step 1: Make a ratio table.

Step 2: Write an ordered pair for each row of the table.

Step 3: Plot the ordered pairs and join the points with a line. If extended, the line should pass through (0, 0).

5. Graph the ratio.

a) 3 : 2   b) 2 : 5   c) 1 : 4   d) 4 : 1   e) 5 : 3   f) 7 : 6

6. A plane flies 1,000 km every hour.

a) Complete the ratio table for the situation.

Time (h)	Distance (km)	Ordered pair
1	1,000	
2		

b) Graph the ratio.

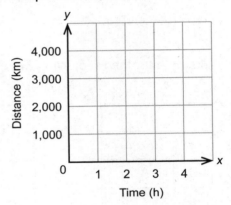

c) Use the graph to tell how far the plane flew in 2.5 hours. _____

7. A train travels 50 miles every hour.

a) Make a ratio table for the situation.

b) Graph the ratio.

c) Extend the line to tell how far the train

   travels in 6 hours. _____

d) A car drives 75 miles every 2 hours. Graph this ratio on the same grid as part b).

e) How far does each vehicle go in 3 hours?

   Train: _____   Car: _____

   Which travels farther in 3 hours, the train or the car? _____

f) What travels faster, the car or the train? How do you know?

g) How can you find the answers to parts e) and f) from the graph?

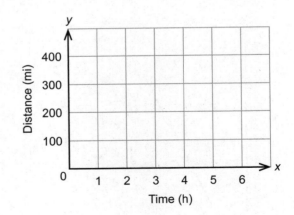

32. Proportional Relationships

1. Circle the ratio tables.

2	5
4	10

3	8
12	2

2	5
4	7

6	8
12	16

3	5
6	15

4	9
12	27

> Two quantities are **proportional** if the table comparing their values is a ratio table.

2. a) Is the distance traveled by the car proportional to the time? Write "yes" or "no."

i)

Time (h)	Distance (km)
1	50
2	100
3	150

ii)

Time (h)	Distance (m)
1	20
2	35
3	50

iii)

Time (h)	Distance (mi)
1	40
2	80
3	120

_____   _____   _____

b) Graph the relationships in part a). Use the given number to skip count on the *y*-axis.

i) 50 km   ii) 20 m   iii) 40 mi

c) Join the points on each graph in order.

d) Predict which lines will pass through the origin if extended. Explain your prediction.

e) Extend the line on each graph until it intersects the *y*-axis. Which lines pass through the origin? Was your prediction in part c) correct?

> A **formula** is an equation that shows how to calculate one quantity from another.
>
> Example: There are 3 triangles for every 1 square.
>
> Formula: number of triangles = 3 × number of squares
>
>
>
> We can use variables such as *t* for the number of triangles and *s* for the number of squares to shorten the formula: $t = 3 \times s$ or $t = 3s$.

3. Complete the table for the formula. Then circle the table if *s* and *t* are proportional.

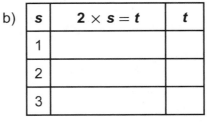

a)

s	4 × s = t	t
1	4 × 1 = 4	4
2	4 × 2 = 8	8
3	4 × 3 = 12	12

b)

s	2 × s = t	t
1		
2		
3		

c)

s	3 × s = t	t
3		
5		
7		

4. Complete the table for the formula. Then circle the table if s and t are proportional.

a)

s	$s + 4 = t$	t
1	$1 + 4 = 5$	5
2		
3		
4		

b)

s	$s + 2 = t$	t
1		
2		
3		
4		

c)

s	$s - 1 = t$	t
3		
6		
10		
4		

5. Predict which formulas show a proportional relationship based on your answers to Questions 3 and 4. Check your answers to parts a) and c) using a table.

a) $s = 3t$

b) $5 \times t = s$

c) $2 + s = t$

d) $y = 7x$

e) $y = x - 7$

f) $a = b \times 6$

6. Complete the table for the formula. Then circle the table if s and t are proportional.

a)

s	$4 \times s - 3 = t$	t
1	$4 \times 1 - 3 = 4 - 3 = 1$	1
2		
3		
4		

b)

s	$2 \times s + 6 = t$	t
1		
2		
3		
4		

c)

s	$2 \times s - 1 = t$	t
1		
2		
3		
4		

d)

s	$3 \times s + 3 = t$	t
1		
2		
3		
4		

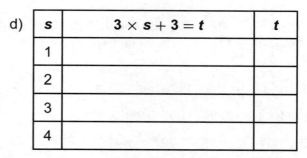

An equation shows a proportional relationship if you get one quantity by *multiplying* the other quantity by a constant (a number). This number is called the **constant of proportionality**.

Example: In the equation $t = 3 \times s$, the constant of proportionality is 3.

7. Find the constant of proportionality.

a) $s = 3t$ _____

b) $5 \times t = s$ _____

c) $9 \times s = t$ _____

d) $y = 60x$ _____

e) $y = 0.7x$ _____

f) $a = b$ _____

8. a) Fill in the table. Then write a formula for the number of blocks in the figures.

i)

Figure 1   Figure 2   Figure 3

Figure Number (n)	Number of Blocks (b)
1	2
2	4
3	6

Formula: _____ $b = 2 \times n$ or $2n$ _____

ii)

Figure 1   Figure 2   Figure 3

Figure Number (n)	Number of Blocks (b)
1	
2	
3	

Formula: _____

iii)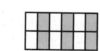

Figure 1   Figure 2   Figure 3

Figure Number (n)	Number of Blocks (b)
1	4
2	
3	

Formula: _____

iv)

Figure 1   Figure 2   Figure 3

Figure Number (n)	Number of Blocks (b)
1	
2	
3	

Formula: _____

b) Are the numbers of blocks and the figure numbers proportional in each table? _____

c) Use the formula to find the number of blocks in Figure 100.

   i) $b =$ ___ $2 \times n$ ___   ii) $b =$ _____   iii) $b =$ _____   iv) $b =$ _____

   $=$ _____ $=$ _____ $=$ _____ $=$ _____

d) Which pattern will have the largest number of blocks in Figure 100? _____

   Which pattern has the largest constant of proportionality? _____

 e) Why should your answers in part d) be the same?

Bonus ▶ Which will be larger, the number of blocks in the 100th figure in the pattern $b = 2 \times n$, or the number of blocks in the 50th figure in the pattern $b = 4 \times n$? Explain.

---

9. a) Use the figure number (*n*) to write a formula for the number of shaded blocks (*s*), and a formula for the total number of blocks (*b*).

i)

Figure 1   Figure 2   Figure 3

Number of shaded blocks: *s* = ___2n___

Total number of blocks: *b* = ___2n + 1___

ii)

Figure 1   Figure 2   Figure 3

Number of shaded blocks: *s* = _____

Total number of blocks: *b* = _____

iii)

Figure 1   Figure 2   Figure 3

Number of shaded blocks: *s* = _____

Total number of blocks: *b* = _____

iv)

Figure 1   Figure 2   Figure 3

Number of shaded blocks: *s* = _____

Total number of blocks: *b* = _____

b) Look at the two formulas you wrote for each pattern in part a). Which quantity is proportional to the figure number (*n*): the number of shaded blocks (*s*)

or the total number of blocks (*b*)? _____

c) Which operations are involved in the formulas that show proportional relationships? Which operations are involved in the formulas that do not show proportional relationships?

10. Circle the part that is proportional to *n* in the expression.

a) $2 \times n + 3$ b) $3n - 1$ c) $5 \times n$ d) $4 + 2.5 \times n - 3$

REMINDER: If a company charges a flat fee of $25 to rent a boat and an hourly rate of $30, the total cost of renting the boat for *h* hours is $30h + 25$ dollars.

---

11. a) Write a formula for the cost *C* to rent a boat for *h* hours.

i) hourly rate: $10	ii) hourly rate: $20	iii) hourly rate: $0	iv) hourly rate: $12.50
flat fee: $20	flat fee: $10	flat fee: $25	flat fee: $0
cost: _____	cost: _____	cost: _____	cost: _____

b) Circle the formula that shows a proportional relationship.

c) For the cost to be proportional to the hourly rate, what should the flat fee be? Explain.

33. Proportional Relationships and Graphs

To graph an equation:

Step 1: Make a table of values.

Step 2: Write an ordered pair for each row of the table.

Step 3: Plot the points.

1. a) Graph the formula, paying attention to the scale on the axes. Join the points in order.

i) $y = 2x - 1$

x	Calculating y	y	Ordered Pair
1	$y = 2(1) - 1 = 1$	1	(1, 1)
2			
3			
4			

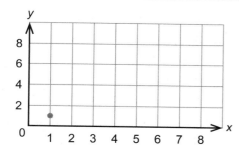

ii) $y = x + 1$

x	Calculating y	y	Ordered Pair
1			
2			
3			
4			

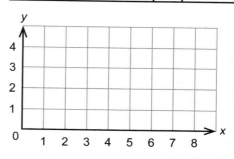

iii) $y = 0.5x$

x	Calculating y	y	Ordered Pair
2			
4			
6			

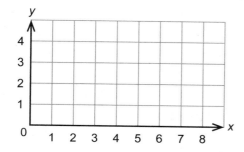

iv) $y = 3x$

x	Calculating y	y	Ordered Pair
1			
2			
3			

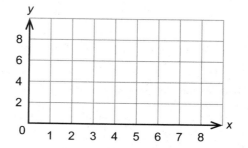

b) Which equations from part a) show proportional relationships? _____

c) Extend each graph in part a) so that it intersects at least one axis.

d) How are the graphs of the proportional relationships different from the other graphs?

2. a) Fill in the table.

Equation	$y = 2x$	$5x = y$	$y = 10x$	$y = 0.6x$
Is this a proportional relationship?	yes			
If $x = 0$, $y = $?	$y = 2(0) = 0$			
(x, y)	(0, 0)			

b) Explain why the graph of a proportional relationship always passes through the origin.

_____

_____

_____

3. a) Make a table for each equation.

A. $y = 2x$

x	y	(x, y)
0	0	(0, 0)
1	2	(1, 2)
2	4	
3	6	

B. $y = 3x$

x	y	(x, y)
0		
1		
2		
3		

C. $y = 4x$

x	y	(x, y)

b) Plot the points and join them in order. Label the lines A, B, and C.

c) Which equation has the largest constant of proportionality? _____

d) Which line is the steepest? _____

e) Predict: The line for the equation $y = 2.5x$ will be steeper than

line _____ but less steep than line _____.

f) Make a table for $y = 2.5x$ and plot the points.

x	y	(x, y)
2		
4		

g) Was your prediction from part e) correct? _____

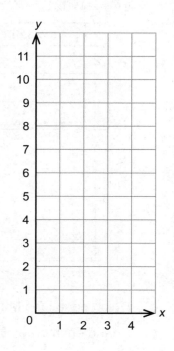

4. a) Two tickets cost $3.

   i) Write a ratio for this situation. _____

   ii) Make a ratio table. Plot the ordered pairs.
        Join the points in order.

Number of Tickets	Cost ($)	Ordered Pair
2		
4		
6		

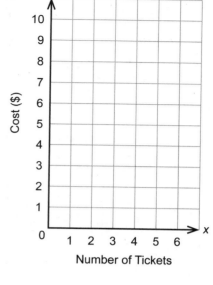

   iii) Plot the point that shows the price of 1 ticket.
         Label the point *A*.

         How much does 1 ticket cost? _____

   b) A rocket flies 3 miles in 2 seconds.

   i) Write a ratio for this situation. _____

   ii) Make a ratio table. Plot the ordered pairs.
        Join the points in order.

Time (s)	Distance (mi)	Ordered Pair

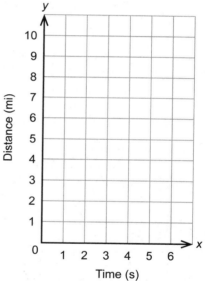

   iii) Plot the point that shows the distance the rocket traveled
         in 1 second. Label it *B*.

         How far did the rocket travel? _____

   c) Plot the point (4.5, 6.75) on the graph in part a). Label it *C*.

   d) Plot the point (4.5, 6.75) on the graph in part b). Label it *D*.

   e) One point, *C* or *D*, has no meaning on the graph. Which one? Explain.

   _____

   _____

5. Draw a graph for the situation. Then answer the questions.

   a) Kathy runs 2 km in 10 minutes. At the same speed, how far will she run in 25 minutes?
       In 1 minute? How long will it take her to run 3 km?

   b) Carlos earns $15 in 2 hours. How much will he earn in 30 minutes? In 5 hours?
       How long will it take him to earn $52.50?

34. Functions as Machines

1. For each input, find the output.

a) **Input:** 3

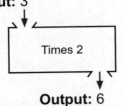

Times 2

Output: 6

Input	Output
3	6
2	
−5	
0	

b) **Input:** 3

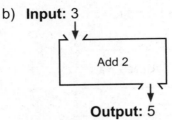

Add 2

Output: 5

Input	Output
3	5
0	
7	
−4	

c) **Input:** 1

Subtract the input from 10

Output: 9

Input	Output
1	9
2	
3	
4	

d) **Input:** Sam

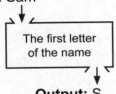

The first letter of the name

Output: S

Input	Output
Sam	S
Megan	
Kim	
John	

e) **Input:** 1

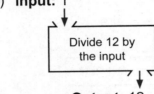

Divide 12 by the input

Output: 12

Input	Output
1	12
2	
3	
4	

f) **Input:** 2

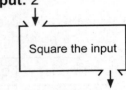

Square the input

Output: 4

Input	Output
2	4
3	
−2	
0	

g) **Input:** triangle

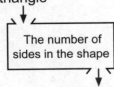

The number of sides in the shape

Output: 3

Input	Output
triangle	3
rectangle	
hexagon	
rhombus	

h) **Input:** 1

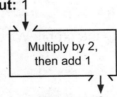

Multiply by 2, then add 1

Output: 3

Input	Output
1	3
2	
3	
4	

i) **Input:** −2

Absolute value of the input

Output: 2

Input	Output
−2	2
1.7	
0	
2	

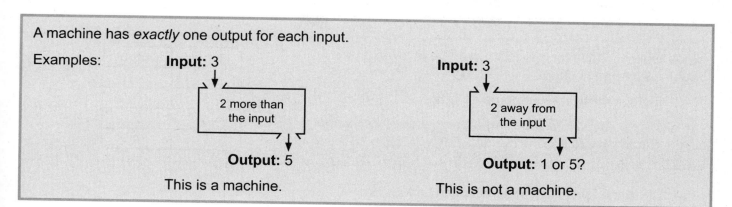

A machine has *exactly* one output for each input.

Examples:

Input: 3
→ 2 more than the input →
Output: 5
This is a machine.

Input: 3
→ 2 away from the input →
Output: 1 or 5?
This is not a machine.

2. Test with any input number to see if the picture shows a machine. Circle the machines.

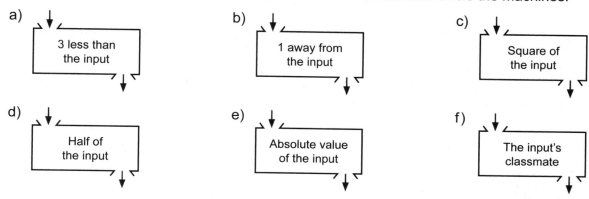

a) 3 less than the input

b) 1 away from the input

c) Square of the input

d) Half of the input

e) Absolute value of the input

f) The input's classmate

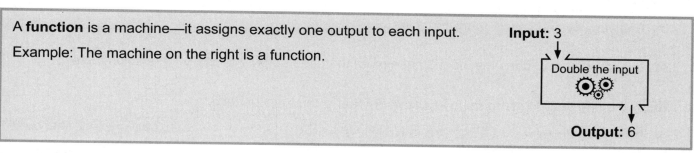

A **function** is a machine—it assigns exactly one output to each input.

Example: The machine on the right is a function.

Input: 3
→ Double the input →
Output: 6

3. Write the rule, then find the output for each input in the table.

a) **Input:** 3
→ Add 2 to the input →
Output: 5

Rule: __add 2__

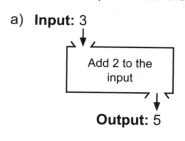

Input	Output
3	5
4	
0	
−2	

b) **Input:** 5
→ Square the input →
Output: 25

Rule: _____

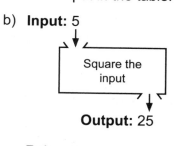

Input	Output
5	25
3	
0	
−3	

c) **Input:** 2
→ Multiply the input by 2, then add 1 →
Output: 5

Rule: _____

Input	Output
2	5
4	
−4	
0	

35. Tables and Functions

Sally makes a table for a function with the following rule:
Subtract 3 from the input.

The inputs are the first four prime numbers.

This is an example of a **function table**, because each input in the table has exactly one output.

Input	Output
2	−1
3	0
5	2
7	4

1. a) Circle the table if it is not a function table.

i)

Input	Output
−2	3
1	6
2	7
4	9

ii)

Input	Output
0	2
1	3
2	4
2	5

iii)

Input	Output
1	2
2	−3
3	1
4	1

iv)

Input	Output
0	0
1	3
2	6
3	9

v)

Input	Output
5	1
3	−2
2	2
3	3

vi)

Input	Output
1	−1
2	0
3	4
3	2^2

b) Explain why part iii) is a function table. _____

c) In part vi) above, does the input 3 have more than one output? Is part vi) a function table?

2. Apply the rule to fill in the missing inputs or outputs in the function table.

a) Rule: Multiply by 3

Input	Output
−1	−3
0	
1	
2	

b) Rule: Divide by 2

Input	Output
4	2
10	
6	
−2	

c) Rule: Multiply by 2, then add 1

Input	Output
−2	
0	
1	
2	

d) Rule: Divide by −3

Input	Output
6	
	1
	0
−9	

e) Rule: Add −0.5

Input	Output
3	2.5
	2
−3	
	−2

f) Rule: Divide by 5, then add 2

Input	Output
5	
10	
−5	
−10	

3. The function was made by addition, subtraction, multiplication, or division. Find the rule.

a)

Input	Output
0	1
1	2
2	3
3	4

Rule: _____

b)

Input	Output
1	10
3	30
5	50
7	70

Rule: _____

c)

Input	Output
−2	−1
0	0
2	1
4	2

Rule: _____

d)

Input	Output
5	1
10	6
15	11
20	16

Rule: _____

e)

Input	Output
1	0.5
2	1.5
3	2.5
4	3.5

Rule: _____

f)

Input	Output
1	4
2	3
3	2
4	1

Rule: _____

4. Find the rule, then complete the function table.

a) Rule: _____

Input	Output
1	4
2	8
3	12
4	
5	
6	

b) Rule: _____

Input	Output
1	−3
2	−2
3	−1
4	
5	
6	

c) Rule: _____

Input	Output
1	1
2	4
3	9
4	
5	
6	

d) Rule: _____

Input	Output
1	0.5
2	1
3	1.5
4	
5	
6	

e) Rule: _____

Input	Output
1	−1
2	−2
3	−3
4	
5	
6	

Bonus ▶ Rule: _____

Input	Output
one	2
two	1
three	2
four	2
five	
six	

5. Make a function table for the rule, "Double the input, then add 3" using the inputs 0, 1, 2, and 3.

36. Sequences and Functions

1. Extend the sequence. Start by finding the gap (the difference between each number and the next).

a) 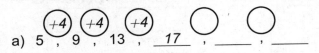 5 , 9 , 13 , _17_ , _____ , _____

b) 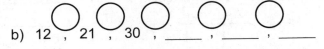 12 , 21 , 30 , _____ , _____ , _____

c) 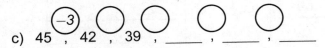 45 , 42 , 39 , _____ , _____ , _____

d) 83 , 77 , 71 , _____ , _____ , _____

e) 14 , 18.5 , 23 , _____ , _____ , _____

f) 35 , 32.5 , 30 , _____ , _____ , _____

g) 10 , 10 , 10 , _____ , _____ , _____

h) 5 , 0 , −5 , _____ , _____ , _____

i) 12 , 31 , 50 , _____ , _____ , _____

j) 104 , 89 , 74 , _____ , _____ , _____

2. Extend the sequence using the given rule.

a) Add 11:   2, 13, _____, _____, _____

b) Subtract 7:   52, 45, _____, _____, _____

c) Add −5:   32, 27, _____, _____, _____

d) Multiply by −1: 6, −6, _____, _____, _____

e) Subtract 1.5: 9, _____, _____, _____

f) Add $\frac{1}{3}$:   1, $1\frac{1}{3}$, _____, _____, _____

g) Add 3.5:   52, _____, _____, _____

h) Subtract −3:   11, 14, _____, _____, _____

i) Add 0.7:   2, 2.7, _____, _____, _____

j) Double: 1, 2, _____, _____, _____

> Look at the sequence: 1, 3, 5, 7, 9, 11, 13, 15, 17
>
> The first term is 1, the second term is 3, the third term is 5, and so on.

3. Find the given term in the sequence in the box above.

a) The 4th term is _____.

b) The 9th term is _____.

c) The 6th term is _____.

d) The 7th term is _____.

4. The first term of a sequence is 1. The second term is also 1, and every other term is the sum of the two previous terms. Write the first 6 terms of the sequence.

Bonus ▶ Is 144 in the sequence?

The position of a term in a sequence is called the **term number**.

Example: 2, 4, 6, 8, 10, 12, 14, 16, 18

        10 is the 5th term in this sequence, so the term number of 10 is 5.

5. A function inputs term numbers and outputs this sequence:
5, 8, 11, 14, 17, 20, 23, 24, 27, 30, 33, 36, 39

For the given term number (the input), write the output.

5 ⟶ _17_   8 ⟶ _____   4 ⟶ _____   9 ⟶ _____   11 ⟶ _____

6. Make a table for the sequence.

a) 2, 5, 8, 11, 14

Term Number	Output
1	2
2	5
3	8
4	
5	

b) 17.5, 15, 12.5, 10, 7.5

Term Number	Output
1	17.5
2	
3	
4	
5	

c) 73, 61, 41, 50, 51

Term Number	Output
1	73
2	
3	
4	
5	

7. Circle the tables in Question 6 that are function tables. Are all of them function

tables? _____ Explain why. _____

A **sequence table** is a special kind of function table with term numbers as inputs: 1, 2, 3, 4, and so on. You can think of the sequence as a set of ordered pairs (Term Number, Term).

Example: **2, 5, 8, 11, 14** ⟶ (1, **2**), (2, **5**), (3, **8**), (4, **11**), (5, **14**)

Any set of ordered pairs is called a **relation**.

8. Change the sequence into a set of ordered pairs.

a) 1, 3, 5, 7, 9

(1, 1), (2, 3), (3, 5), (4, 7), (5, 9)

c) 4, 7, 10, 13, 16

b) 2, 4, 6, 8, 10

(1,   ), (2,   ), (3,   ), (4,   ), (5,   )

d) 3, 7, 11, 15, 19

9. Change the set of ordered pairs into a sequence of numbers.

a) (1, 0), (2, 4), (3, 8), (4, 12), (5, 16)

b) (1, 17), (2, 11), (3, 9), (4, 4), (5, 1)

c) (1, 2), (2, 3), (3, 4), (4, 3), (5, 2)

d) (1, 5), (2, 9), (3, 5), (4, 9), (5, 5), (6, 9), (7, 5), (8, 9)

10. a) The pairs are not in order. Reorder them so that the first numbers are in order.

   i) (4, 4), (6, 2), (2, 9), (3, 6), (1, 10), (5, 3)   ii) (4, 7), (2, 6), (5, 6), (1, 2), (6, 5), (3, 8)

   iii) (2, 4), (5, 7), (4, 4), (1, 7), (6, 4), (3, 7), (7, 7)   iv) (3, 7), (5, 9), (1, 5), (6, 10), (4, 8), (2, 6)

b) Match each sequence in part a) to a description below.

   increases, then decreases _____   increases by the same amount _____

   repeats _____   decreases by different amounts _____

> Remember: A function assigns exactly one output to each input. You can think of a function as a set of ordered pairs (input, output) in which no input has more than one output.
>
> Examples: (1, 3), (2, 6), (3, 9), (4, 12)   (1, 5), (2, 6), (2, 7), (3, 9)
>
>   This is a function.   This is not a function.

11. Make a table for the set of ordered pairs. Do the ordered pairs represent a function?

a) (1, 2), (2, 3), (2, 4), (3, 5), (4, 6), (5, 7)

Input	Output
1	2
2	3, 4
3	5
4	6
5	7

_____*not a function*_____

b) (1, 1), (2, 2), (3, 3), (4, 4), (5, 5)

Input	Output
1	
2	
3	
4	
5	

_____

c) (1, −3), (3, 2), (2, 3), (5, 2), (4, 11)

Input	Output
1	
2	
3	
4	
5	

_____

d) (2, 3), (1, 2), (3, 4), (4, 5), (5, 6), (3, 1)

Input	Output
1	
2	
3	
4	
5	

_____

e) (1, 5), (2, 5), (3, 5), (4, 5), (5, 5)

f) (1, 1), (3, 4), (2, 0), (5, 7), (3, 2), (4, 3)

37. Functions and Mapping Diagrams

1. For the set of ordered pairs, draw arrows between the corresponding input and output.

a) (1, 2), (2, 4), (3, 3), (4, 5), (5, 1)

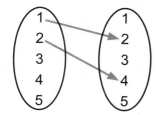

b) (1, 3), (2, 4), (1, 4), (4, 6), (6, 2)

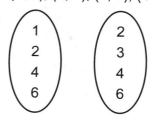

c) (1, 2), (2, 3), (3, 4), (4, 3), (5, 2)

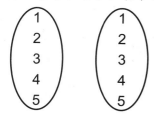

d) (1, 4), (2, 7), (3, 4), (4, 7), (5, 4)

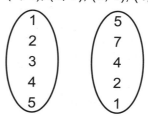

e) (1, −1), (2, −2), (3, −3), (4, −4), (5, −5)

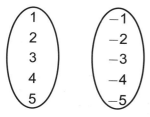

f) (1, a), (2, w), (9, w), (4, p), (6, n)

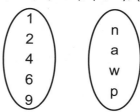

To draw a **mapping diagram** from a table of inputs and outputs, write all the different inputs on the left and all the different outputs on the right.

Then draw arrows between the corresponding input and output.

Input	Output
1	3
7	21
10	30
20	60

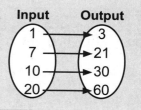

---

2. Draw a mapping diagram for the table.

a)

Input	Output
1	2
2	3
3	4
4	5

b)

Input	Output
1	1
2	0
3	1
4	0

c)

Input	Output
New York	USA
Paris	France
Boston	USA
Toronto	Canada

d)

Input	Output
Europe	UK
Europe	Italy
Asia	India
Africa	Nigeria

You can use a diagram to show any relation.

Example: (1, 5), (3, 2), (5, −1), (−1, −1), (3, 6)

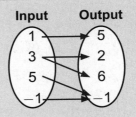

3. Draw a diagram for the relation.

a) (1, 2), (2, 4), (3, 6), (4, 8), (5, 10)

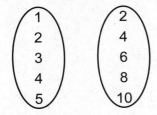

b) (1, 3), (2, 4), (1, 4), (4, 6), (6, 2)

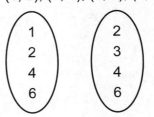

c) (1, 2), (2, 3), (3, 4), (4, 3), (5, 2)

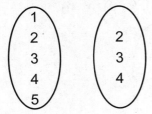

d) (1, 4), (2, 7), (3, 4), (4, 7), (5, 4)

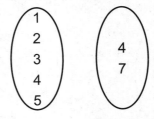

e) (1, 2), (2, 4), (3, 3), (4, 5), (5, 1)

f) (1, 3), (2, 4), (9, 4), (4, 6), (2, 5)

To determine if a diagram represents a function, check if more than one arrow goes from one input. If an input has more than one corresponding output, then the diagram does not represent a function.

Examples:

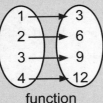
function

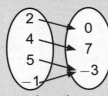
function

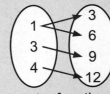
not a function

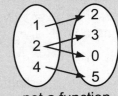
not a function

4. Circle the diagrams that represent a function.

A.
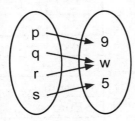

B.
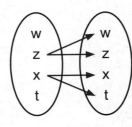

C.
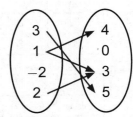

D.

5. Which diagrams in Question 3 represent a function? _____

JUMP Math Accumula

38. Sequences and Graphs

To graph a sequence:

Step 1: Make a list of ordered pairs.

2, 4, 6, 8, 10

↓

(1, **2**), (2, **4**), (3, **6**), (4, **8**), (5, **10**)

Step 2: Plot the ordered pairs on a graph.

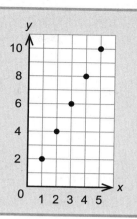

1. a) Graph the sequence of numbers by first making a list of ordered pairs.

i) 1, 4, 6, 12

(1,   ), (2,   ), (3,   ), (4,   )

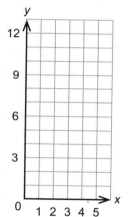

ii) 3, 6, 9, 12

(1,   ), (2,   ), (3,   ), (4,   )

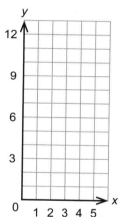

iii) 1, 4, 7, 10

(1,   ), (2,   ), (3,   ), (4,   )

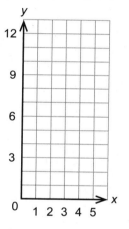

iv) 2, 3, 4, 9

(1,   ), (2,   ), (3,   ), (4,   )

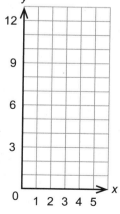

v) 11, 9, 7, 5

(1,   ), (2,   ), (3,   ), (4,   )

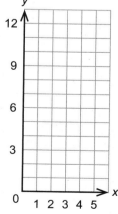

vi) 12, 10, 8, 4

(1,   ), (2,   ), (3,   ), (4,   )

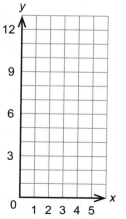

b) Look at your graphs from part a). Can the points be joined by a straight line?

i) _____   ii) _____   iii) _____   iv) _____   v) _____   vi) _____

A sequence is **linear** if plotting the points on a graph and joining them make a straight line.
If a sequence is not linear, we call it **nonlinear**.

Examples: 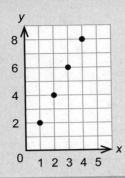 2, 4, 6, 8 is a
linear sequence.

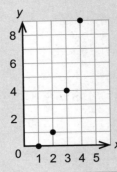 0, 1, 4, 9 is a
nonlinear sequence.

2. a) For the sequence table, find the gaps between the terms.

i)
Term Number	Term
1	3
2	5
3	7
4	9

ii)
Term Number	Term
1	10
2	7
3	4
4	1

iii)
Term Number	Term
1	1
2	4
3	9
4	10

b) Plot the ordered pairs from each table in part a) on a graph.

i)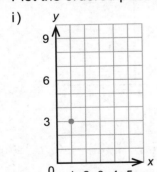

ii)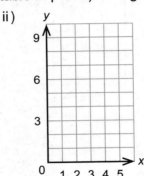

iii)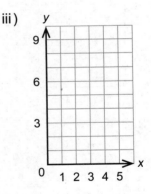

c) Which sequences from part a) are linear?

d) Which sequences from part a) have a gap that is always the same?

e) What do you notice from parts c) and d)?

REMINDER: In an **increasing sequence**, each number is greater than the one before it.
In a **decreasing sequence**, each number is less than the one before it.

3. a) Write the sequence for each table in Question 2, part a).

b) Which sequences from part a) are increasing?

c) Which sequences from part a) always have a positive gap?

d) What do you notice from parts b) and c)?

JUMP Math Accumula

4. On grid paper, graph the increasing sequence.

    a) 5, 7, 9, 11   b) 2, 3, 7, 9   c) 1, 4, 9, 16

5. On grid paper, graph the decreasing sequence.

    a) 12, 8, 4, 0   b) 11, 5, 3, 2   c) 15, 12, 7, 0

6. Write if the graph represents an increasing, decreasing, and/or linear sequence.

a)
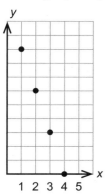

    decreasing linear

b)
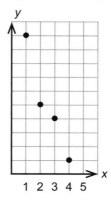

c)
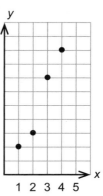

When the gap is …	always positive	always negative	always the same
The sequence is …	increasing	decreasing	linear

7. Find the gap and write the correct description for the sequence table.

a)

Term Number	Term
1	9
2	7
3	5
4	3

−2, −2, −2

    decreasing linear

b)

Term Number	Term
1	2
2	5
3	6
4	8

c)

Term Number	Term
1	0
2	2
3	4
4	6

d)

Term Number	Term
1	1
2	2
3	3
4	4

e)

Term Number	Term
1	1
2	4
3	9
4	16

f)

Term Number	Term
1	5
2	3
3	1
4	0

39. Functions and Algebra

1. Evaluate the expressions for each value of x.

x	$3x - 1$	$2x + 3$	$2x - 1$
1	$3x - 1 = 3(1) - 1$ $= 3 - 1$ $= 2$		
2	$= 3(2) - 1$ $=$ $=$		
3			
4			

Mathematicians usually use the variable x for the input and y for the output.

Example: In this set of ordered pairs (x, y), for each value of x, there is exactly one output. $y = 2x + 1$ represents the **rule** of the **function**.

x	$y = 2x + 1$
1	3
2	5
3	7
4	9

2. Complete the function table.

a)
x	$y = x - 1$
1	
2	
3	
4	

b)
x	$y = -x + 2$
1	
2	
3	
4	

c)
x	$y = \dfrac{1}{2}x$
1	
2	
3	
4	

d)
x	$y = 4$
1	
2	
3	
4	

e)
x	$y = -2x$
1	
2	
3	
4	

f)
x	$y = x^2$
1	
2	
3	
4	

3. Finish the function table, write the ordered pairs, and plot the ordered pairs on the graph.

a)

x	2x + 2
1	
2	
3	
4	

(1,   ), (2,   ), (3,   ), (4,   )

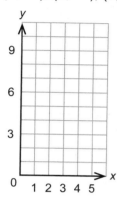

b)

x	3x − 2
1	
2	
3	
4	

(1,   ), (2,   ), (3,   ), (4,   )

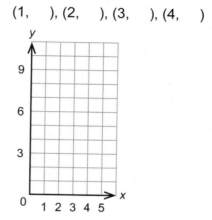

c)

x	−3x + 13
1	
2	
3	
4	

(1,   ), (2,   ), (3,   ), (4,   )

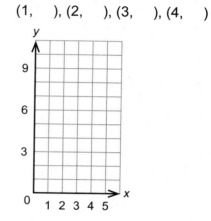

d)

x	−2x + 3
1	
2	
3	
4	

(1,   ), (2,   ), (3,   ), (4,   )

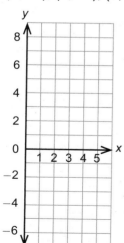

e)

x	0.5x + 2
1	
2	
3	
4	

(1,   ), (2,   ), (3,   ), (4,   )

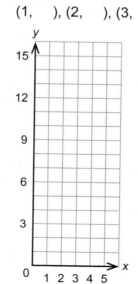

f)

x	$x^2 - 1$
1	
2	
3	
4	

(1,   ), (2,   ), (3,   ), (4,   )

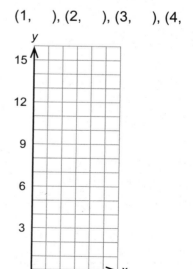

4. a) Determine the coefficient of *x*. Remember, a coefficient is a number used to multiply a variable. Fill in the table using the equation. Find the gap.

i) $y = 2x + 1$

x	y
1	3
2	5
3	
4	

(+2)

coefficient of *x* = __2__

gap = __+2__

ii) $y = 2x - 1$

x	y
1	
2	
3	
4	

coefficient of *x* = _____

gap = _____

iii) $y = -2x + 5$

x	y
1	
2	
3	
4	

coefficient of *x* = _____

gap = _____

iv) $y = \dfrac{1}{2}x + 1$

x	y
1	1.5
2	2
3	
4	

coefficient of *x* = _____

gap = _____

v) $y = -0.5x + 1$

x	y
1	
2	
3	
4	

coefficient of *x* = _____

gap = _____

vi) $y = -3x - 2$

x	y
1	
2	
3	
4	

coefficient of *x* = _____

gap = _____

b) Where do you see the gap in the expression? _____

5. a) Plot each function table in Question 4.a) on a graph. Use grid paper for parts iv), v), and vi).

i)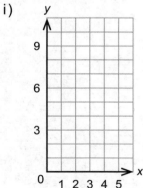

ii)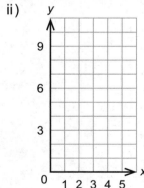

iii)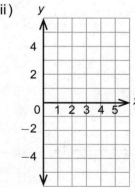

b) Which graphs from part a) are increasing? _____ Which have a positive coefficient? _____

c) Which graphs from part a) are decreasing? _____ Which have a negative coefficient? _____

d) How can you tell from the coefficient if the graph is increasing or decreasing? _____

_____

40. Formulas for Tables

1. Use the gap to complete the table.

a)

Input	Output
1	3
2	
3	
4	

+2
+2
+2

b)

Input	Output
1	4
2	
3	
4	

+2
+2
+2

c)

Input	Output
1	5
2	
3	
4	

−3
−3
−3

d)

Input	Output
1	1
2	
3	
4	

+4
+4
+4

2. a) Use the rule to fill in the table. Find the gap between outputs.

i) Rule: Multiply by 3 and add 1

Input	Output
1	
2	
3	
4	

gap = _____

ii) Rule: Multiply by 0.5 and add 2

Input	Output
1	
2	
3	
4	

gap = _____

iii) Rule: Multiply by −2 and add 10

Input	Output
1	
2	
3	
4	

gap = _____

iv) Rule: Multiply by 0 and subtract 4

Input	Output
1	
2	
3	
4	

gap = _____

b) Compare the gap and the rule for each table in part a). What do you notice?

_____

_____

To find the rule for how to get the output from the input:

Step 1: Find the gap between the numbers in the Output column.

Input (*n*)	*n* × gap	Output
1		5
2		8
3		11

+3
+3

Step 2: Multiply each Input by the gap.

Input (*n*)	*n* × gap	Output
1	3	5
2	6	8
3	9	11

+3
+3

Step 3: What must you add (or subtract) to each number in the second column to get the output?

Input (*n*)	*n* × gap	Output
1	3	5
2	6	8
3	9	11

+3
+3

Add 2

Step 4: Write the rule for the table. Rule: Multiply the input by 3, then add 2.

3. Use the steps above to find the rule for the table.

a)

Input (*n*)	*n* × gap	Output
1		11
2		15
3		19

Add _____

Rule: Multiply by _____, then add _____.

b)

Input (*n*)	*n* × gap	Output
1		5
2		7
3		9

Add _____

Rule: Multiply by _____, then add _____.

c)

Input (*n*)	*n* × gap	Output
1		2
2		5
3		8

Subtract _____

Rule: Multiply by _____, then subtract _____.

d)

Input (*n*)	*n* × gap	Output
1		4
2		10
3		16

Subtract _____

Rule: Multiply by _____, then subtract _____.

4. Write the sequence for each table in Question 3.

a) *11, 15, 19*

b)

c)

d)

Which sequences are increasing? _____

110

JUMP Math Accumula

5. Use the gap in the sequence to find the coefficient in the formula. Then complete the chart to finish writing the formula.

a)

Input (*n*)	*n* × gap	Output
1	5	2
2	10	7
3	15	12
4	20	17

+5
+5
+5

−3

Formula: __5*n* − 3__

b)

Input (*n*)	*n* × gap	Output
1		1
2		4
3		7
4		10

Formula: _____

c)

Input (*n*)	*n* × gap	Output
1		3
2		7
3		11
4		15

Formula: _____

d)

Input (*n*)	*n* × gap	Output
1		9
2		15
3		21
4		27

Formula: _____

Once you know the gap—and hence the coefficient—you really only need to see how the first term compares to the gap in order to find the formula.

Example: In Question 5.a), the gap is 5 and the first output is 2, so the formula is 5*n* − 3.

---

6. Find the gaps in the sequence. Then write the formula for the sequence.

a) 3 , 5 , 7 , 9

Formula: _____

b) 9 , 20 , 31 , 42

Formula: _____

c) 12 , 17 , 22 , 27

Formula: _____

d) 2, 3.5, 5, 6.5

e) 53, 55, 57, 59

Bonus ▶ 10, 7, 4, 1

---

7. a) Write a formula for the number of toothpicks in the sequence shown below:

Figure 1   Figure 2   Figure 3   Figure 4

b) Use your formula to determine the number of toothpicks in the 30th figure.

41. Sequences, Graphs, and Algebra

1. Without writing the sequence for the rule, find the gap in the sequence.

   a) Start at 15. Subtract 4 each time. __−4__

   b) Start at 3. Add 2 each time. _____

   c) Start at 15. Add 3.5 each time. _____

   d) Start at 23. Subtract 2 each time. _____

2. Without writing the sequence for the formula, find the gap in the sequence. Remember to include the sign.

   a) $3n + 2$ b) $5 - 4n$ c) $6 + 2n$ d) $5 - 3n$ e) $0.5n + 4$

   _____   _____   _____   _____   _____

3. a) The sequence in the graph is nonlinear. Write the term values of the graph, and then find the gaps.

   __0__ ____ ____ ____

   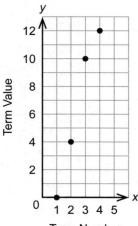

   b) Do the gaps show the difference between the term values

   or the term numbers? _____

   c) Should you look at the horizontal axis or the vertical axis to

   see the gaps between the terms of the sequence? _____

4. a) Without writing the sequence for the graph, find the gap in the sequence.

   i)   ii)   iii)

   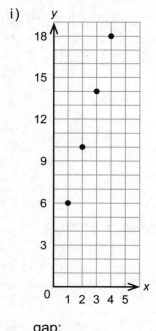   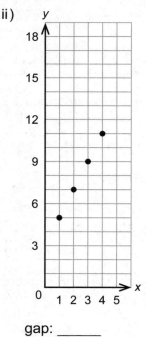   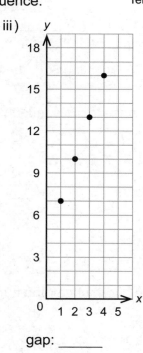

   gap: _____   gap: _____   gap: _____

   b) Sara wrote the formula for each graph in part a), but the graphs got mixed up! Match the graph to the formula.

      $3n + 4$ _____ $4n + 2$ _____ $2n + 3$ _____

5. **a)** The expression represents a sequence. Evaluate the expression with $n = 1$ to find the first term of the sequence.

    i) $3n + 4$ _____

    ii) $3n + 2$ _____

    iii) $3n - 1$ _____

b) Each graph represents a sequence. Find the term value when the term number is 1.

A.

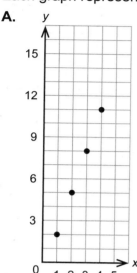

B.

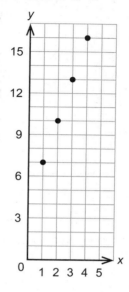

C.

_____   _____   _____

c) Match each expression from part a) with a graph from part b).

    i) $3n + 4$ _____

    ii) $3n + 2$ _____

    iii) $3n - 1$ _____

6. Match the graph to the formula.

A.

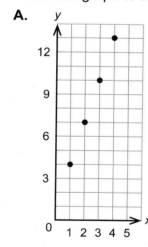

B.

C.

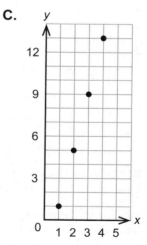

  a) $3n - 2$ _____   b) $4n - 3$ _____   c) $3n + 1$ _____

7. **a)** Finish writing the expressions below with numbers of your choice.

    $3n +$ _____ $2n +$ _____ $4n +$ _____ $3n +$ _____ $2n +$ _____

  b) Draw a graph for each expression from part a) on grid paper in random order.

  c) Have a partner match the expressions to the graphs.

42. Linear Functions

1. The graph is linear. Join the points with a straight line to find the missing values in the table.

a)
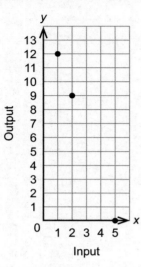

Input	Output
1	12
2	9
3	
	3
5	

b)
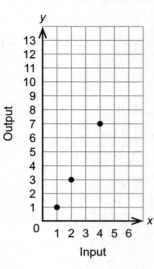

Input	Output
1	1
	3
4	7
5	
	13

2. Extend the line to find the output when the input is 11.

a)
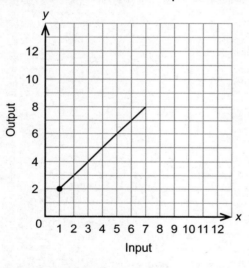

When the input is 11, the output is _____.

b)
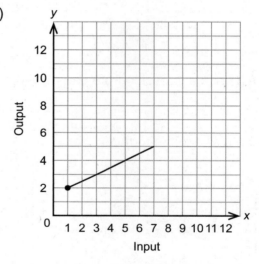

When the input is 11, the output is _____.

In a linear function, any number can be the input, not just a whole number.

3. For each graph in Question 1, find the missing values in the table.

a)

Input	Output
0	
1.5	
2.5	
3.5	
4.5	

b)

Input	Output
0.5	
1.5	
2.5	
4.5	
5.5	

                     JUMP Math Accumula

4. Extend the line to find the output for each input.

a)

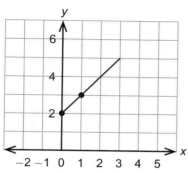

Input	1	0	−1	−2
Output	3			

b)

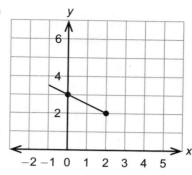

Input	2	0	−1	−2
Output	2			

5. A car is traveling at a constant speed of 60 km/h.

a) Write an expression for the distance the car traveled after t hours.

_____

b) Create a table of values for the distance the car traveled after t hours.

t hours	Distance Traveled (km)

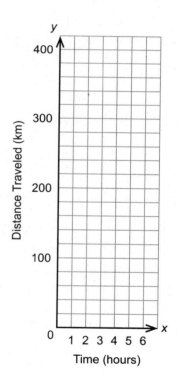

c) Write the ordered pairs from the above table of values. Then plot the points on the graph on the right. _____

d) Join the points on the graph with a straight line. If the car traveled for 3.5 hours, how far would it go? _____

e) How many hours would it take the car to travel 390 km? Extend the line to find out. _____

6. a) For the function, plot a graph for x equal to 1, 2, 3, 4, and 5. Note: Leave extra space on the horizontal axis to extend the graph.

　i) $y = 4x + 1$ 　　　　　 ii) $y = 5x − 2$ 　　　　　 iii) $y = 3x + 9$

b) Extend the line on each graph from part a) to find y when $x = 6$. Then check your answer by substituting $x = 6$ in the formula.

c) Use the graphs to find the value of x when $y = 33$.

d) Write an equation and solve it to check your work for part c). Example: Solve $4x + 1 = 33$ to check your answer to part i).

43. Rate of Change

Change in *x* is the horizontal change from the first point to the second point along the *x*-axis.

Change in *y* is the vertical change from the first point to the second point along the *y*-axis.

Example: From point *A* to point *B*: change in *x* = 2, change in *y* = −3

Change in *x* and change in *y* can be negative numbers.

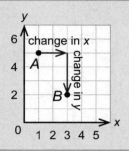

1. Find the change in *x* and the change in *y* from point *A* to point *B*.

a)
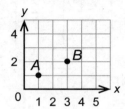

change in *x* = _____

change in *y* = _____

b)
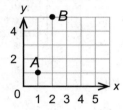

change in *x* = _____

change in *y* = _____

c)
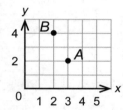

change in *x* = _____

change in *y* = _____

d)
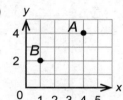

change in *x* = _____

change in *y* = _____

e)
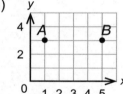

change in *x* = _____

change in *y* = _____

f)
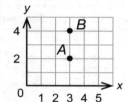

change in *x* = _____

change in *y* = _____

2. Find the change in *x* and the change in *y* from point *A* to point …

a)
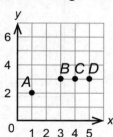

b)
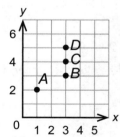

a)
i) *B*: change in *x* = ____, change in *y* = ____

ii) *C*: change in *x* = ____, change in *y* = ____

iii) *D*: change in *x* = ____, change in *y* = ____

b)
i) *B*: change in *x* = ____, change in *y* = ____

ii) *C*: change in *x* = ____, change in *y* = ____

iii) *D*: change in *x* = ____, change in *y* = ____

c) The change in _____ from point *A* to any point on a horizontal line is constant.

d) The change in _____ from point *A* to any point on a vertical line is constant.

3. Write the coordinates of points *A* and *B* in the table, then find the change in *x* and the change in *y* by finding the gaps.

a)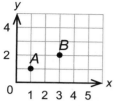

x	y
1	1
3	2

+2 ... +1

change in *x* = _____

change in *y* = _____

b)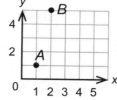

x	y

change in *x* = _____

change in *y* = _____

c)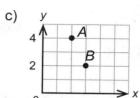

x	y

change in *x* = _____

change in *y* = _____

d)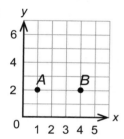

x	y

change in *x* = _____

change in *y* = _____

e)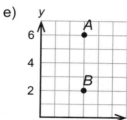

x	y

change in *x* = _____

change in *y* = _____

f)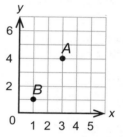

x	y

change in *x* = _____

change in *y* = _____

The **rate of change** is the rate of change in *y* to change in *x*. Rate of change $= \dfrac{\text{change in } y}{\text{change in } x}$

The rate of change is very important in mathematics and other sciences.

4. Find the rate of change from *A* to *B*.

a)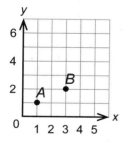

$\dfrac{\text{change in } y}{\text{change in } x} = \dfrac{1}{2}$

b)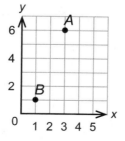

$\dfrac{\text{change in } y}{\text{change in } x} = \underline{} =$

c)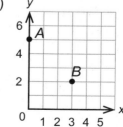

Rate of change $= \underline{} =$

5. Find the rate of change in Question 4 from *B* to *A*.

a) $\dfrac{\text{change in } y}{\text{change in } x} = \dfrac{-1}{-2} = \dfrac{1}{2}$

b) $\dfrac{\text{change in } y}{\text{change in } x} = \underline{\hspace{1cm}}$

c) $\dfrac{\text{change in } y}{\text{change in } x} = \underline{\hspace{1cm}} =$

d) What did you notice in parts a), b), and c)? _____

> The rate of change from *A* to *B* is equal to the rate of change from *B* to *A*, so we can call this:
>
> ### The rate of change between *A* and *B*

6. Find the rates of change between point *A* and the other points on the graph. Reduce to lowest terms.

a)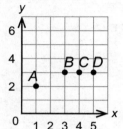

b)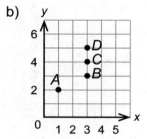

c)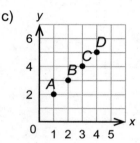

a)
B: $\dfrac{\text{change in } y}{\text{change in } x} = \underline{\hspace{1cm}}$

C: $\dfrac{\text{change in } y}{\text{change in } x} = \underline{\hspace{1cm}}$

D: $\dfrac{\text{change in } y}{\text{change in } x} = \underline{\hspace{1cm}}$

b)
B: $\dfrac{\text{change in } y}{\text{change in } x} = \underline{\hspace{1cm}}$

C: $\dfrac{\text{change in } y}{\text{change in } x} = \underline{\hspace{1cm}}$

D: $\dfrac{\text{change in } y}{\text{change in } x} = \underline{\hspace{1cm}}$

c)
B: $\dfrac{\text{change in } y}{\text{change in } x} = \underline{\hspace{1cm}}$

C: $\dfrac{\text{change in } y}{\text{change in } x} = \underline{\hspace{1cm}}$

D: $\dfrac{\text{change in } y}{\text{change in } x} = \underline{\hspace{1cm}}$

d) For the graph in part a), circle the biggest rate of change.

    A to *B*   *A* to *C*   *A* to *D*

e) For the graph in part b), circle the biggest rate of change.

    A to *B*   *A* to *C*   *A* to *D*

f) What did you notice in graph c)? _____

g) For the graph in part a), what is the rate of change between points *B* and *D*?

$\dfrac{\text{change in } y}{\text{change in } x} = \underline{\hspace{1cm}} =$

What did you notice? _____

Bonus ▶ Explain why you cannot find the rate of change between points *B* and *D* in part b). _____

_____

44. Slope in Linear Functions

Mathematicians use other terms when they work with linear functions or straight lines.

Another name for the change in *x* is **run**.
Another name for the change in *y* is **rise**.

Another name for rate of change is **slope**, so slope = $\dfrac{\text{rise}}{\text{run}}$.

Example: From point *A* to point *B*, run = 2 and rise = 3, so the slope is $\dfrac{3}{2}$.

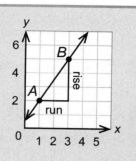

1. Find the rise and run from point *A* to point *B*. Then find the slope and reduce to lowest terms.

a)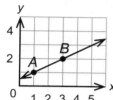

slope = $\dfrac{\text{rise}}{\text{run}}$ = ——

b)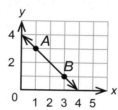

slope = $\dfrac{\text{rise}}{\text{run}}$ = ——

c)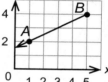

slope = $\dfrac{\text{rise}}{\text{run}}$ = ——

d)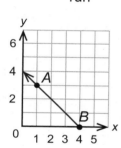

slope = $\dfrac{\text{rise}}{\text{run}}$ = ——

e)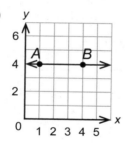

slope = $\dfrac{\text{rise}}{\text{run}}$ = ——

f)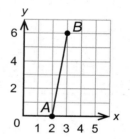

slope = $\dfrac{\text{rise}}{\text{run}}$ = ——

2. Find the slopes of the lines *AB*, *AC*, and *AD*. Reduce to lowest terms.

a)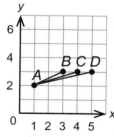

slope of *AB* = $\dfrac{\text{rise}}{\text{run}}$ = ——

slope of *AC* = $\dfrac{\text{rise}}{\text{run}}$ = ——

slope of *AD* = $\dfrac{\text{rise}}{\text{run}}$ = ——

b)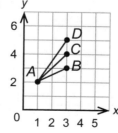

slope of *AB* = $\dfrac{\text{rise}}{\text{run}}$ = ——

slope of *AC* = $\dfrac{\text{rise}}{\text{run}}$ = ——

slope of *AD* = $\dfrac{\text{rise}}{\text{run}}$ = ——

c)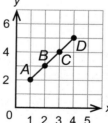

slope of *AB* = $\dfrac{\text{rise}}{\text{run}}$ = ——

slope of *AC* = $\dfrac{\text{rise}}{\text{run}}$ = ——

slope of *AD* = $\dfrac{\text{rise}}{\text{run}}$ = ——

3. a) For the graph in Question 2.a), find the slope of a new line, *BD*.

$$\text{slope of } BD = \frac{\text{rise}}{\text{run}} = \underline{\hspace{2cm}}$$

b) Can you find the slope of a new line, *BD*, in Question 2.b)? _____

For any horizontal line, rise = 0, so the slope of a horizontal line is 0.

For any vertical line, run = 0.

Mathematicians don't define the slope of the vertical line because we cannot divide a number by 0.

---

4. Write the coordinates of points *A* and *B* in the table. Then find the rise and run by finding the gaps. Then find the slope of the line *AB*. Reduce to lowest terms.

a)

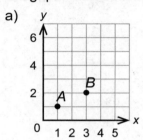

	x	y	
+2	1	1	+1
	3	2	

run = _____   rise = _____

$$\text{slope} = \frac{\text{rise}}{\text{run}} = \underline{\hspace{1cm}}$$

b)

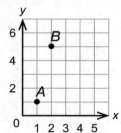

	x	y	

run = _____   rise = _____

$$\text{slope} = \frac{\text{rise}}{\text{run}} = \underline{\hspace{1cm}}$$

c)

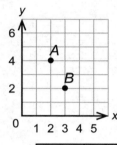

	x	y	

run = _____   rise = _____

$$\text{slope} = \frac{\text{rise}}{\text{run}} = \underline{\hspace{1cm}}$$

d)

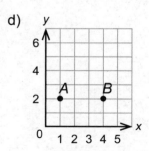

	x	y	

run = _____   rise = _____

$$\text{slope} = \frac{\text{rise}}{\text{run}} = \underline{\hspace{1cm}}$$

e)

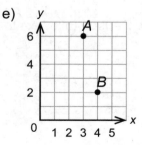

	x	y	

run = _____   rise = _____

$$\text{slope} = \frac{\text{rise}}{\text{run}} = \underline{\hspace{1cm}}$$

f)

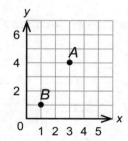

	x	y	

run = _____   rise = _____

$$\text{slope} = \frac{\text{rise}}{\text{run}} = \underline{\hspace{1cm}}$$

5. Find the slope of a line that passes through the pair of points by filling in the table and finding the gaps.

a) $A\,(1, 2),\ B\,(2, 5)$

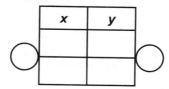

$$\text{slope} = \frac{\text{rise}}{\text{run}} = \frac{3}{1} = 3$$

b) $A\,(3, 1),\ B\,(4, 2)$

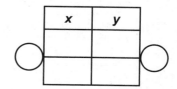

$$\text{slope} = \frac{\text{rise}}{\text{run}} = \frac{\quad}{\quad} =$$

c) $A\,(5, 2),\ B\,(3, 3)$

$$\text{slope} = \frac{\text{rise}}{\text{run}} = \frac{\quad}{\quad} =$$

d) $A\,(0, 4),\ B\,(4, 2)$

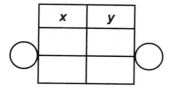

$$\text{slope} = \frac{\text{rise}}{\text{run}} = \frac{\quad}{\quad} =$$

e) $A\,(2, 0),\ B\,(0, 2)$

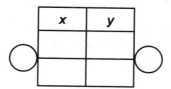

$$\text{slope} = \frac{\text{rise}}{\text{run}} = \frac{\quad}{\quad} =$$

f) $A\,(3, 4),\ B\,(7, 4)$

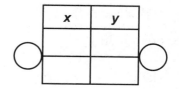

$$\text{slope} = \frac{\text{rise}}{\text{run}} = \frac{\quad}{\quad} =$$

g) $A\,(-1, 3),\ B\,(2, 6)$

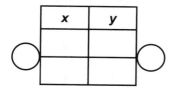

$$\text{slope} = \frac{\text{rise}}{\text{run}} = \frac{\quad}{\quad} =$$

h) $A\,(3, -2),\ B\,(2, 0)$

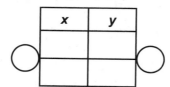

$$\text{slope} = \frac{\text{rise}}{\text{run}} = \frac{\quad}{\quad} =$$

i) $A\,(-1, -2),\ B\,(-3, -5)$

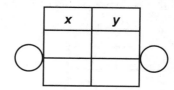

$$\text{slope} = \frac{\text{rise}}{\text{run}} = \frac{\quad}{\quad} =$$

6. Find the rise and run by finding the change in y and the change in x. Then find the slope.

a) $A\,(-2, 1),\ B\,(0, -3)$

rise $= -3 - 1 = -4$

run $= 0 - (-2) = 2$

$$\text{slope} = \frac{\text{rise}}{\text{run}} = \frac{-4}{2} =$$

b) $A\,(2, -1),\ B\,(1, 2)$

rise $=$

run $=$

$$\text{slope}\ \frac{\text{rise}}{\text{run}} = \frac{\quad}{\quad} =$$

c) $A\,(-2, -1),\ B\,(-4, -5)$

rise $=$

run $=$

$$\text{slope}\ \frac{\text{rise}}{\text{run}} = \frac{\quad}{\quad} =$$

7. a) Find the slope of the line on the graph.

i) slope of $AB = \dfrac{\text{rise}}{\text{run}} = \underline{\quad}$ ii) slope of $AC = \dfrac{\text{rise}}{\text{run}} = \underline{\quad}$

b) Mark the point $D\,(5, 6)$ on the graph and find the slope of the line AD.

slope of $AD = \dfrac{\text{rise}}{\text{run}} = \underline{\quad} =$

c) Are the slopes between every two points on this straight line equal? _____

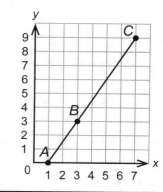

45. Finding Slope Using Tables and Equations

1. Fill in the table using the rule. Find the changes in *x* and *y* and then find the slope.

a) Multiply by 2.5 and add 1.

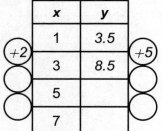

x	*y*
1	3.5
3	8.5
5	
7	

change in *x* = __+2__

change in *y* = __+5__

slope = $\dfrac{5}{2}$ = 2.5

b) Multiply by 3 and add 1.5.

x	*y*
−1	−1.5
1	
3	
5	

change in *x* = _____

change in *y* = _____

slope = —— =

c) Multiply by 1.5 and subtract 2.

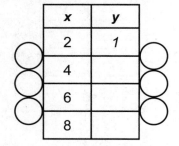

x	*y*
2	1
4	
6	
8	

change in *x* = _____

change in *y* = _____

slope = —— =

d) Where can you find the slope in a rule? _____

2. Fill in the table using the equation. The change in *x* is 1. Find the change in *y* and the slope.

a) $y = 2x + 1$

x	*y*
1	3
2	5

coefficient of *x*: __2__

slope = $\dfrac{2}{1}$ = 2

b) $y = 2x - 1$

x	*y*
1	
2	

coefficient of *x*: _____

slope = —— =

c) $y = 3x - 2.5$

x	*y*
1	0.5
2	

coefficient of *x*: _____

slope = —— =

d) $y = -2x + 1$

x	*y*
1	−1
2	

coefficient of *x*: _____

slope = —— =

e) $y = -3x + 3$

x	*y*
1	
2	

coefficient of *x*: _____

slope = —— =

f) $y = 1.5x - 1$

x	*y*
1	
2	

coefficient of *x*: _____

slope = —— =

g) Where can you find the slope in the rule? _____

3. According to ski trail difficulty ratings in North America, ski slopes are rated by level of difficulty, as shown below:

Beginner hills: $\dfrac{6}{100}$ to $\dfrac{25}{100}$ Intermediate hills: $\dfrac{25}{100}$ to $\dfrac{40}{100}$ Advanced hills: $\dfrac{40}{100}$ to $\dfrac{100}{100}$

Find the slope and say if the hill is for beginner, intermediate, or advanced skiers.

a)
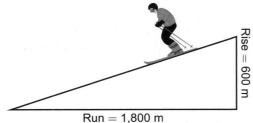
Run = 1,800 m   Rise = 600 m

_____

b)
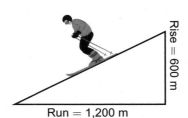
Run = 1,200 m   Rise = 600 m

_____

c)
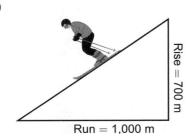
Run = 1,000 m   Rise = 700 m

_____

d)
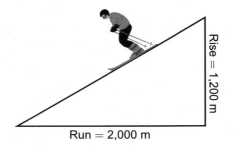
Run = 2,000 m   Rise = 1,200 m

_____

e)

Run = 3,000 m   Rise = 600 m

_____

f)
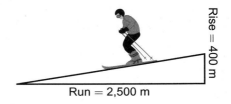
Run = 2,500 m   Rise = 400 m

_____

4. a) The four different linear functions below are represented in different ways. Calculate the slope for each.

i)

Input	Output
−1	1
0	2
1	3
2	4

ii)
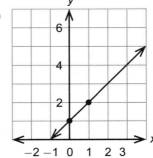

iii) $y = 3x - 4$

iv) (1, 1), (2, 3), (3, 5), (4, 7)

b) Which has the greatest slope? Are there any with the same slope?

5. A balloon is released from the top of a tower. The graph shows the height of the rising balloon over time.

a) What is the height of the tower? _____

b) Find the slope of the line.

c) Use the slope to find the height of the balloon after 65 seconds.

d) Check your answer to part c) using the graph.

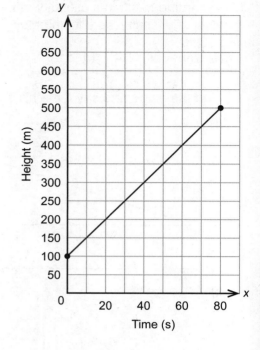

6. A ramp in California must have a maximum rise of 1 foot for a 12-foot horizontal run.

a) Find the maximum slope.

b) An exit door is 3 feet higher than the ground level. Determine the horizontal run needed for a ramp.

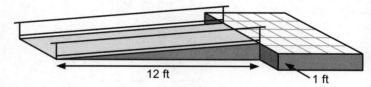

7. A shed has a square base and each side measures 15 feet. The roof has a $\frac{1}{6}$ slope. Find the maximum height of the shed roof from the ground.

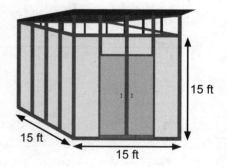

8. A ramp slopes upward from the sidewalk to the entrance of a building. The horizontal run of the ramp is 28 ft from the sidewalk. Find the maximum height of the ramp, if the ramp is 2 ft high when it is 8 ft from the sidewalk.

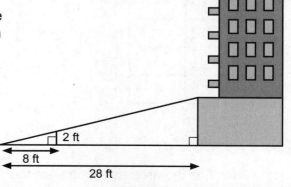

46. Coordinate Plane—Four Quadrants

We can extend both axes on a coordinate grid to include negative numbers. The axes divide the grid into four **quadrants**. We use **Roman numerals** to number the quadrants: 1 = I, 2 = II, 3 = III, 4 = IV.

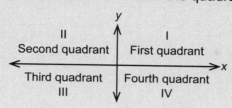

1. a) Label the origin (O) and the x- and y-axes.

   b) Label both axes with positive and negative integers. Count by 1s.

   c) Number the four quadrants (using I, II, III, IV).

   d) Which quadrants are these points in?

   A (3, 3) ___*I*___ B (−3, −2) _____

   C (−3, 3) _____ D (3, −2) _____

   Bonus ▶ Point E has coordinates (−154, −238).

   Which quadrant is it in? _____

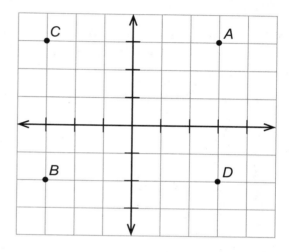

2. In Figure 1, point A (2, 3) is in the first quadrant. Its x- and y-coordinates are both positive.

   a) Find the coordinates of these points.

   P (,   ) Q (,   )

   R (,   ) S (,   )

   b) Plot and label these points.

   B (3, 2) C (1, 4) D (4, 1)

3. In Figure 1, point F (−2, 3) is in the second quadrant. Its x-coordinate is negative and its y-coordinate is positive.

   a) Find the coordinates of these points.

   K (,   ) L (,   )

   M (,   ) N (,   )

   b) Plot and label these points.

   G (−3, 2) H (−1, 6) I (−4, 1)

Figure 1

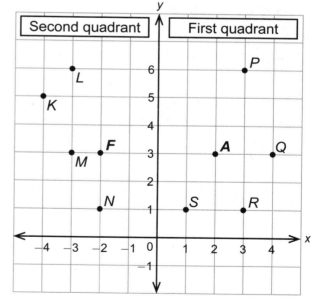

4. In Figure 2, point *A* (−2, −3) is in the third quadrant. Its x- and y-coordinates are both negative.

a) Find the coordinates of these points.

K (,   ) L (,   )

M (,   ) N (,   )

b) Plot and label these points.

B (−3, −4) C (−2, −6) D (−4, −3)

5. In Figure 2, point *F* (2, −3) is in the fourth quadrant. Its x-coordinate is positive and its y-coordinate is negative.

a) Find the coordinates of these points.

P (,   ) Q (,   )

R (,   ) S (,   )

b) Plot and label these points.

G (3, −4) H (1, −6)

I (4, −1) J (1, −2)

6. In Figure 3, points *B* (2, 0) and *C* (−4, 0) are both on the x-axis. The y-coordinate of any point on the x-axis is zero.

a) Find the coordinates of these points.

P (,   ) Q (,   )

b) Plot and label these points.

A (4, 0) M (−2, 0)

7. In Figure 3, points *D* (0, 2) and *E* (0, −3) are both on the y-axis. The x-coordinate of any point on the y-axis is zero.

a) Plot and label these points.

G (0, 4) H (0, −1)

b) Find the coordinates of these points.

K (,   ) L (,   )

Figure 2

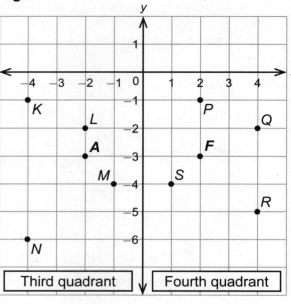

Figure 3

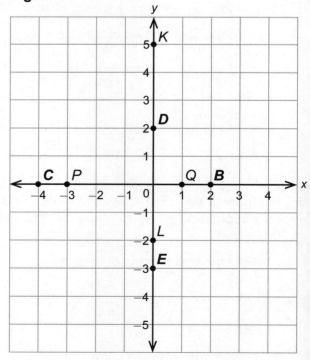

8. a) Find the coordinates of these points.

P (,   )   Q (,   )

R (,   )   S (,   )

T (,   )   U (,   )

V (,   )   W (,   )

b) Plot and label these points.

A (3, 4)   B (5, −2)

C (−3, −2)   D (−4, 1)

E (3, 0)   F (0, 2)

G (0, −3)   H (−5, 0)

c) Plot and label these points.
Hint: Use a ruler to estimate for decimals and fractions.

I (4.5, 2.5) $J\left(-2\frac{1}{2}, 3\frac{1}{2}\right)$

$K\left(-3.5, -4\frac{1}{4}\right)$ $L\left(3\frac{1}{3}, -3\frac{2}{3}\right)$

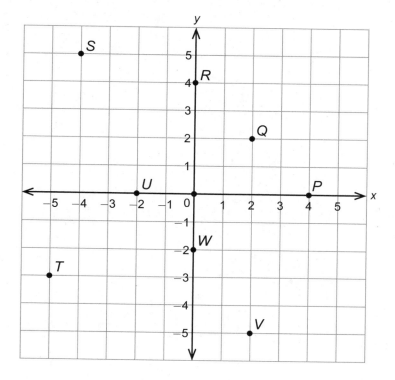

9. a) Plot the set of points.

i) (6, −4), (6, −2), (6, 0), (6, 1), (6, 3)

ii) (−3, −4), (−3, −2), (−3, 0), (−3, 2)

iii) (−6, 5), (−3, 5), (0, 5), (5, 5)

b) Draw a line that joins the points in each set in part a). Label each line.

c) Fill in the table for each set of points and the line.

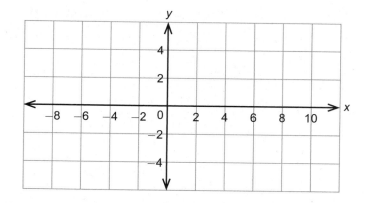

	i)	ii)	iii)
Which axis is the line parallel to?			
Which coordinate changes?			
Which coordinate stays the same?			
Write the coordinates for another point on the line where it extends beyond the grid.			
Bonus ▶ Write an equation for the line.	$x = 6$		

47. Distance Between Points on a Vertical or Horizontal Line

> reminder: When subtracting integers, $2 - 3 = 2 + (-3)$ and $2 - (-3) = 2 + (+3)$.

1. Do both subtractions. Then circle the subtraction that tells you how far apart the integers are on the number line.

   a) $3 - 2 = \underline{\quad 1 \quad}$

   $2 - 3 = \underline{\quad -1 \quad}$

   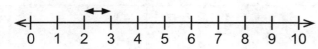

   b) $7 - 4 = \underline{\qquad}$

   $4 - 7 = \underline{\qquad}$

   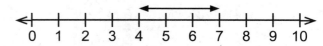

   c) $(+2) - (-4) = \underline{\qquad}$

   $(-4) - (+2) = \underline{\qquad}$

   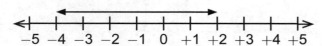

   d) $(-2) - (-5) = \underline{\qquad}$

   $(-5) - (-2) = \underline{\qquad}$

2. Which subtraction will give the distance between -3 and $+5$, $(+5) - (-3)$ or $(-3) - (+5)$?

   How do you know? _____

   _____

> A distance is always positive. The **absolute value** of a number is its distance from zero.
>
> The notation $|-3|$ is short for "the absolute value of -3." Examples: $|-3| = 3$ and $|+3| = 3$

3. Write the absolute value.

   a) $|-2| =$ b) $|+4| =$ c) $|-25| =$ d) $|0| =$

   e) $\left|-\dfrac{3}{4}\right| =$ f) $\left|+2\dfrac{1}{7}\right| =$ g) $|+2.76| =$ h) $|-0.6| =$

> The distance between two integers is the absolute value of their difference. Examples:
>
> 4 and 7 are $|4 - 7| = |-3| = 3$ units apart.   2 and (-4) are $|-4 - 2| = |-6| = 6$ units apart.

4. Subtract. Then take the absolute value to find the distance apart.

   a) $|(-6) - (+3)| = |\underline{\ -9\ }| = \underline{\ 9\ }$,

   so -6 and $+3$ are $\underline{\ 9\ }$ units apart.

   b) $|(-4) - (-1)| = |\underline{\qquad}| = \underline{\qquad}$,

   so -4 and -1 are $\underline{\qquad}$ units apart.

   c) $|(+16) - (-5)| = |\underline{\qquad}| = \underline{\qquad}$,

   so $+16$ and -5 are $\underline{\qquad}$ units apart.

   d) $|35 - 200| = |\underline{\qquad}| = \underline{\qquad}$,

   so 35 and 200 are $\underline{\qquad}$ units apart.

5. Use Figure 1 to find the distance between the points.

a) The distance between (2, 0) and (6, 0) is _____ units.

b) The distance between (2, 1) and (6, 1) is _____ units.

c) The distance between (2, 3) and (6, 3) is _____ units.

d) The distance between (2, y) and (6, y) is _____ units.

Figure 1

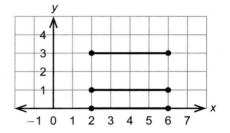

6. Use Figure 2 to find the distance between the points.

a) The distance between (−4, 0) and (2, 0) is _____ units.

b) The distance between (−4, 1) and (2, 1) is _____ units.

c) The distance between (−4, −2) and (2, −2) is _____ units.

d) The distance between (−4, y) and (2, y) is _____ units.

Figure 2

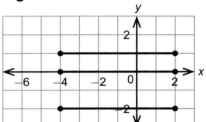

7. Look at your answers to Questions 5 and 6. Does the distance between two points on the same horizontal line depend on the x-coordinate or the y-coordinate?

_____

Points with the same x-coordinate are points on the same vertical line.
Points with the same y-coordinate are points on the same horizontal line.

8. Subtract the x-coordinates and take the absolute value to find the distance between the points.

a) (−3, 0) and (1, 0) _____ units

b) (5, 0) and (−2, 0) _____ units

c) (−1, −10) and (1,−10) _____ units

d) (−8, 6) and (−2, 6) _____ units

Figure 3

9. Use Figure 3 to find the distance between the points.

a) (0, −2) and (0, 5)

_____ units

b) (1, −2) and (1, 5)

_____ units

c) (−2, −2) and (−2, 5)

_____ units

d) (x, −2) and (x, 5)

_____ units

10. Subtract the y-coordinates and take the absolute value to find the distance between the points.

a) (1, −3) and (1, 2) _____ units

b) (1, −5) and (1, 2) _____ units

c) (−1, −2) and (−1, 2) _____ units

d) (−1, −5) and (−1, −2) _____ units

e) (184, −2) and (184, 7) _____ units

f) (−51, 2) and (−51, −5) _____ units

48. Finding the *y*-intercept from a Graph

Remember, to find the rate of change for a line, you can find the slope between any two points, *A* and *B*, on the line.

Step 1: Choose two points. Use integer coordinates if possible.

Step 2: Label the point to the left *A* and find the slope from *A* to *B* so that the run will be positive.

Example: *A* (2, 3) and *B* (4, 2)

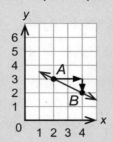

$$\text{run} = 4 - 2 = +2$$
$$\text{rise} = 2 - 3 = -1$$
$$\text{slope} = \frac{\text{rise}}{\text{run}} = \frac{-1}{+2} = -\frac{1}{2}$$

1. Mark points *A* and *B* on the line, then find the slope. Label the point to the left *A*.
   Hint: Use integer coordinates if possible.

a)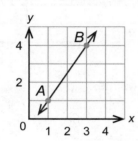

run = _____   rise = _____

$\text{slope} = \dfrac{\text{rise}}{\text{run}} =$ ——

b)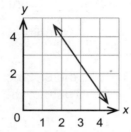

run = _____   rise = _____

$\text{slope} = \dfrac{\text{rise}}{\text{run}} =$ ——

c)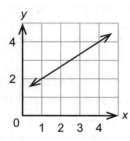

run = _____   rise = _____

$\text{slope} = \dfrac{\text{rise}}{\text{run}} =$ ——

d)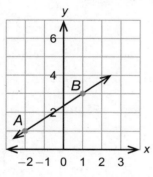

run = __3__   rise = __2__

$\text{slope} = \dfrac{\text{rise}}{\text{run}} =$ ——

e)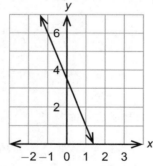

run = _____   rise = _____

$\text{slope} = \dfrac{\text{rise}}{\text{run}} =$ ——

f)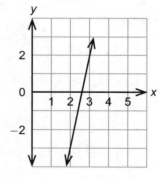

run = _____   rise = _____

$\text{slope} = \dfrac{\text{rise}}{\text{run}} =$ —— =

A line on a graph that goes from bottom left to top right shows an increasing function.
A line on a graph that goes from top left to bottom right shows a decreasing function.

---

2. a) Which linear functions in Question 1 are increasing?

   b) Which linear functions in Question 1 have a positive slope?

   c) How can you tell if a line is increasing or decreasing from its slope?

JUMP Math Accumula

The **y-intercept** is where a line intersects the y-axis.

Examples:

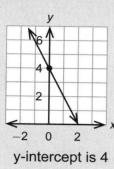

y-intercept is 4

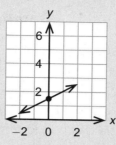

y-intercept is 1.5

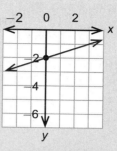

y-intercept is −2

3. a) Extend the line to find the y-intercept. Mark the y-intercept.

i)

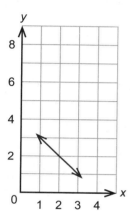

y-intercept: _____

ii)

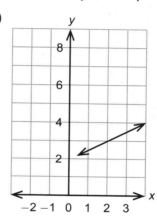

y-intercept: _____

iii)

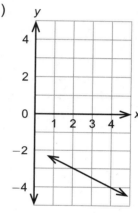

y-intercept: _____

iv)

y-intercept: _____

v)

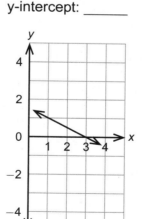

y-intercept: _____

vi)

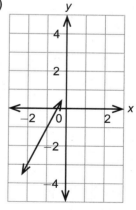

y-intercept: _____

b) Use two points with integer coordinates to find the slope of each line in part a). Do parts iv) to vi) in your notebook. For vi), you will need to find two points with integer x-coordinates.

i) run = _____ rise = _____   ii) run = _____ rise = _____   iii) run = _____ rise = _____

slope = $\frac{rise}{run}$ = ——— =   slope = $\frac{rise}{run}$ = ——   slope = $\frac{rise}{run}$ = ——

c) Do you see any relationship between the slope and the y-intercept of a line? _____

To draw a line with y-intercept $= 3$ and slope $= \dfrac{-1}{2}$:

Step 1

Mark the y-intercept on the y-axis. y-intercept: 3

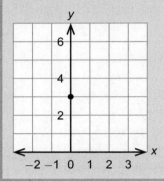

Step 2

$$\text{slope} = \frac{\text{rise}}{\text{run}} = \frac{-1}{2}$$

From the y-intercept, count 2 units to the right (for the run $+2$) and 1 unit down (for the rise -1) to mark the second point.

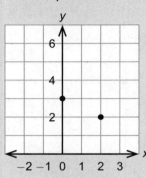

Step 3

Join the points with a straight line, then extend the line.

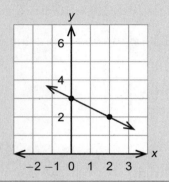

4. Mark the y-intercept, then draw a line with the given y-intercept and slope.

a)

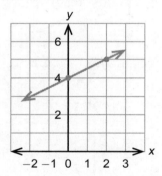

y-intercept $= 4$, slope $= \dfrac{1}{2}$

b)

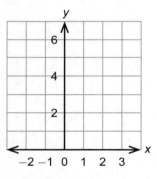

y-intercept $= 3$, slope $= \dfrac{-1}{3}$

c)

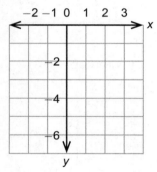

y-intercept $= -3$, slope $= \dfrac{-1}{2}$

d)

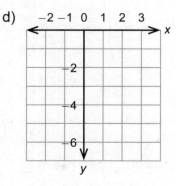

y-intercept $= -3$, slope $= 2$

Hint: Write the slope as $\dfrac{2}{1}$.

e)

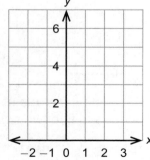

y-intercept $= 5$, slope $= -2$

Hint: Write the slope as $\dfrac{-2}{1}$.

f)

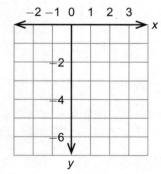

y-intercept $= -2$, slope $= -2$

49. Finding the y-intercept from an Equation

1. a) Fill in the table using the equation, then plot the line. Extend the line to find the y-intercept.

i) $y = 2x - 1$

x	y
1	1
2	3

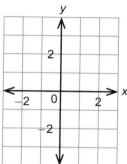

y-intercept: _____

ii) $y = -1.5x + 2$

x	y
1	
2	

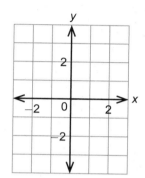

y-intercept: _____

iii) $y = -x - 0.5$

x	y
1	
2	

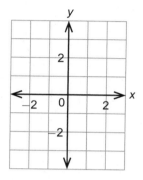

y-intercept: _____

iv) $y = \dfrac{1}{2}x - 3$

x	y
1	$-\dfrac{5}{2} = -2.5$
2	

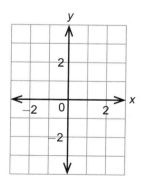

y-intercept: _____

v) $y = -2x + \dfrac{1}{2}$

x	y
1	
2	

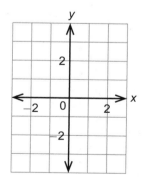

y-intercept: _____

vi) $y = \dfrac{1}{2}x - \dfrac{1}{2}$

x	y
1	
2	

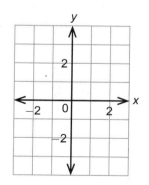

y-intercept: _____

b) Circle the y-intercept in each equation in part a). Remember to include the sign.

2. **a)** Fill in the table using the equation.

i) $y = 2x + 3$

x	y
−1	1
0	3
1	

ii) $y = 1.5x + 4$

x	y
−2	
0	
1	

iii) $y = -2x - 3$

x	y
−1	
0	
2	

b) Plot the line for each equation in part a) and mark the *y*-intercept.

i)

ii)

iii)

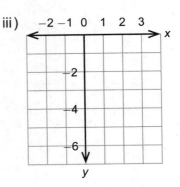

y-intercept: _____   y-intercept: _____   y-intercept: _____

c) Where can you find the y-intercept in the table? _____

3. Find the value of y when x = 0.

a) $y = 3x - 1$

$= 3(0) - 1 = -1$

b) $y = -0.5x + 2$

$=$

c) $y = 2x$

$=$

d) $y = -2x$

$=$

e) $y = 1.5x - 2$

$=$

f) $y = -2.5x + 1$

$=$

4. Make a table for each function in Question 3.

a) $y = 3x - 1$

x	y
1	
2	

b) $y = -0.5x + 2$

x	y
1	
2	

c) $y = 2x$

x	y
1	
2	

d) $y = -2x$

e) $y = 1.5x - 2$

f) $y = -2.5x + 1$

5. **a)** Which functions in Question 4 would have a graph with a line that passes

through (0, 0)? _____

b) For lines that pass through (0, 0) in Question 4, the y-intercept is _____.

6. For each equation in Question 1.a), replace x with 0 to find y. If you don't get the y-intercept, find your mistake.

i) $y = 2x - 1$

$= 2(0) - 1 = -1$

ii) $y = -1.5x + 2$

iii) $y = -x - 0.5$

iv) $y = \frac{1}{2}x - 3$

v) $y = -2x + \frac{1}{2}$

vi) $y = \frac{1}{2}x - \frac{1}{2}$

To find the *y*-intercept from the equation of a line, replace *x* with 0 and find *y*.

7. a) Fill in the table using the equation, then plot the line. Extend the line to find the y-intercept.

i) $y = 2x$

x	y
1	2
2	4

ii) $y = 1.5x$

x	y
1	
2	

iii) $y = -x$

x	y
1	
2	

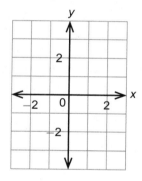

y-intercept: _____

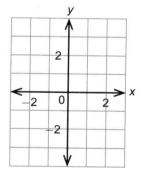

y-intercept: _____

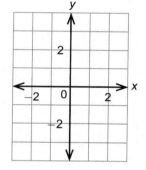

y-intercept: _____

b) Circle the graphs that go through the origin (0, 0).

Remember, lines that go through the origin represent a proportional relationship between x and y. The y-intercept for lines that go through the origin is 0.

8. Circle the tables in Question 7 that represent a proportional relationship between x and y.

9. Circle the equations that represent a proportional relationship.

A. $y = 3x - 2$

B. $y = 2.5x$

C. $y = -3x$

D. $y = \frac{1}{2}x$

E. $y = -1.5x + \frac{1}{2}$

F. $y = -\frac{3}{2}x$

50. Finding the *y*-intercept from a Table

1. a) Use the run and rise to complete the table. Remember, change in x is run, and change in y is rise.

   i)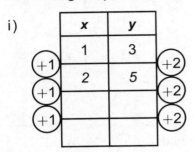

   ii)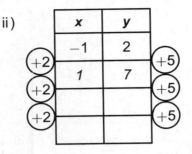

   iii)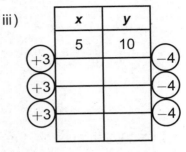

   b) Find the slope for each table in part a) by finding the rise over run.

   i) slope = $\dfrac{\text{rise}}{\text{run}} = \dfrac{2}{1} = 2$

   ii) slope = $\dfrac{\text{rise}}{\text{run}} = \underline{\quad} =$

   iii) slope = $\dfrac{\text{rise}}{\text{run}} = \underline{\quad} =$

2. a) Find the run and rise, then find the slope.

   i)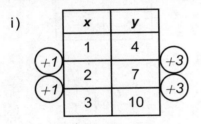

   ii)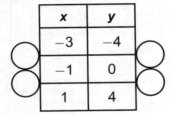

   iii)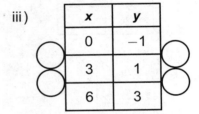

   slope = $\dfrac{\text{rise}}{\text{run}} = \dfrac{3}{1} = 3$

   slope = $\dfrac{\text{rise}}{\text{run}} = \underline{\quad} =$

   slope = $\dfrac{\text{rise}}{\text{run}} = \underline{\quad}$

   b) Continue with the tables from part a). Multiply x by the slope. What must you add or subtract to each number in the second column to get y?

   i)
x	slope × x	y
1	$3 \times 1 = 3$	4
2	$3 \times 2 = 6$	7
3		10

   Add ___1___

   ii)
x	slope × x	y
−3		−4
−1		0
1		4

   Add _____

   iii)
x	slope × x	y
0		−1
3		1
6		3

   Subtract _____

   c)   Write an equation for each table in part b).

   i) y = 3x + 1

   ii) y =

   iii) y =

   d) Circle the y-intercept in each equation in part c).

To write the equation of a line and find the y-intercept from a table:

Step 1: Find the run and rise, then find the slope.

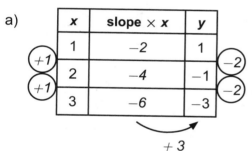

x	slope × x	y
1		2
3		8
5		14

(+2 between x values, +6 between y values)

$$slope = \frac{rise}{run} = \frac{6}{2} = 3$$

Step 2: Multiply each x by the slope.

x	slope × x	y
1	3	2
3	9	8
5	15	14

Step 3: What must you add (or subtract) to each number in the second column to get y?

x	slope × x	y
1	3	2
3	9	8
5	15	14

Subtract 1

Step 4: Write the equation for the table. Substitute x with 0 to find the y-intercept.

$$y = 3x - 1$$

$$y\text{-intercept} = 3(0) - 1 = -1$$

---

3. Find the slope to complete the table and write the equation. Circle the y-intercept.

a)

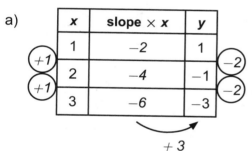

x	slope × x	y
1	−2	1
2	−4	−1
3	−6	−3

(+1 between x values, −2 between y values)

+ 3

$$slope = \frac{rise}{run} = \frac{-2}{1} = -2$$

equation: $y = -2x + 3$ (the +3 is circled)

b)

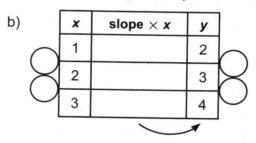

x	slope × x	y
1		2
2		3
3		4

$$slope = \frac{rise}{run} = \underline{\quad} =$$

equation: _____

c)

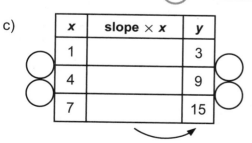

x	slope × x	y
1		3
4		9
7		15

$$slope = \frac{rise}{run} = \underline{\quad} =$$

equation: _____

d)

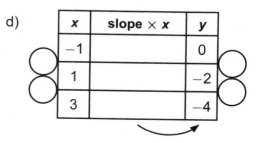

x	slope × x	y
−1		0
1		−2
3		−4

$$slope = \frac{rise}{run} = \underline{\quad} =$$

equation: _____

4. a) Extend the line to find the y-intercept.

A.

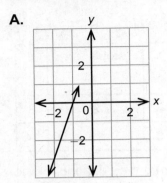

y-intercept: _____

B.

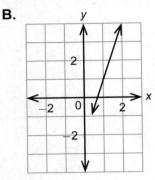

y-intercept: _____

C.

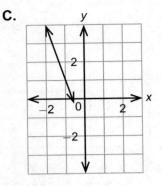

y-intercept: _____

b) Match the graph to the equation.

   i) $y = 3x - 2$ _____

   ii) $y = -3x - 2$ _____

   iii) $y = 3x + 3$ _____

5. a) Match the table to the equation.

A.

x	y
−1	5
0	3
1	1

B.

x	y
−1	1
1	5
2	7

C.

x	y
−2	−7
−1	−5
1	−1

   i) $y = 2x - 3$ _____

   ii) $y = 2x + 3$ _____

   iii) $y = -2x + 3$ _____

b) Circle the y-intercept in each equation.

c) Graph each table in part a), write the equation above the graph, and mark the y-intercept to check your answers to part b).

A. _____

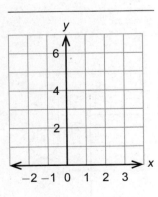

B. _____

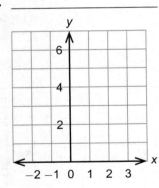

C. _____

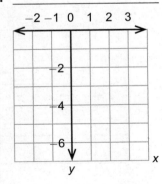

6. a) Finish writing five different equations with numbers of your choice.

   $y = 2x +$ _____ $y = 2x -$ _____ $y = 3x +$ _____ $y = 3x -$ _____ $y = 2x +$ _____

   b) Draw a graph for each of your five equations on grid paper, in random order.

   c) Have a partner match the equations to the graphs.

51. Finding the *y*-intercept from Ordered Pairs

1. a) Graph the list of ordered pairs and join them to make a line. Extend the line to find the *y*-intercept.

i) (1, 3), (2, 5)

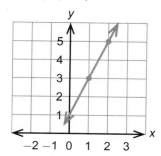

y-intercept: ___1___

ii) (−2, 4), (−1, 3)

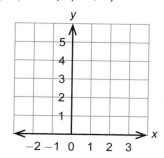

y-intercept: _____

iii) (1, 2), (3, 6)

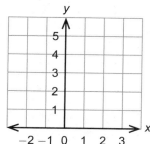

y-intercept: _____

iv) (−2, 2), (1, −4)

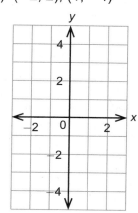

y-intercept: _____

v) (2, 4), (1, 1)

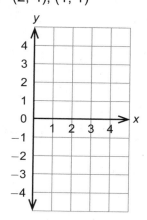

y-intercept: _____

vi) (−1, 3), (1, −3)

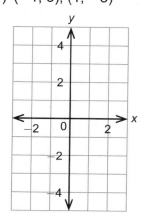

y-intercept: _____

b) Find the slope of each line in part a).

i) $\text{slope} = \dfrac{\text{rise}}{\text{run}} = \dfrac{2}{1} = 2$

ii) $\text{slope} = \dfrac{\text{rise}}{\text{run}} = \underline{\quad} =$

iii) $\text{slope} = \dfrac{\text{rise}}{\text{run}} = \underline{\quad} =$

iv) $\text{slope} = \dfrac{\text{rise}}{\text{run}} = \underline{\quad} =$

v) $\text{slope} = \dfrac{\text{rise}}{\text{run}} = \underline{\quad} =$

vi) $\text{slope} = \dfrac{\text{rise}}{\text{run}} = \underline{\quad} =$

c) Make a table with the coordinates from part a). Use the slope to complete the table and write an equation. Circle the *y*-intercept. Do parts iv) to vi) in your notebook.

i)

x	slope × *x*	*y*
1	2	3
2	4	5

+ 1

equation: ___*y* = 2*x* + 1___

ii)

x	slope × *x*	*y*
−2		4
−1		3

equation: _____

iii)

x	slope × *x*	*y*

equation: _____

To find the *y*-intercept from ordered pairs (1, 4), (3, 10) without graphing:

Step 1
Write the coordinates in a table, then find the run, rise, and slope.

x	slope × x	y
1		4
3		10

+2 ... +6

$$slope = \frac{rise}{run} = \frac{6}{2} = 3$$

Step 2
Multiply each x by the slope.

x	slope × x	y
1	3	4
3	9	10

Step 3
What must you add (or subtract) to the second column to get y?

x	slope × x	y
1	3	4
3	9	10

Add 1

The y-intercept is +1.

2. A line goes through the given points. Find the y-intercept without graphing.

a) (2, −1), (3, −3)

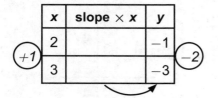

x	slope × x	y
2		−1
3		−3

+1 ... −2

$$slope = \frac{rise}{run} = \frac{-2}{1} = -2$$

y-intercept: _____

b) (1, −4), (3, 2)

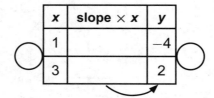

x	slope × x	y
1		−4
3		2

$$slope = \frac{rise}{run} = ——— =$$

y-intercept: _____

c) (−2, 1), (1, 7)

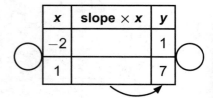

x	slope × x	y
−2		1
1		7

$$slope = \frac{rise}{run} = ——— =$$

y-intercept: _____

3. a) Four linear functions are represented in different ways below. Find the *y*-intercept for each.

A.

x	y
−2	1
−1	0
1	−2
2	−3

B.

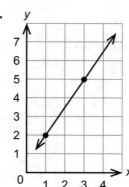

C. (−1, −2), (1, 2), (2, 4)   **D.** y = −3x − 1

b) Which function has the greatest y-intercept?

c) Which function has a negative y-intercept?

d) Which function goes through the origin?

e) Which function represents a proportional relationship between x and y?

52. Writing an Equation of a Line Using the Slope and *y*-intercept

reminder: You can find the slope of a straight line from any two points on the line.

1. **a)** Find the slope of the line $y = 2x + 5$ using different pairs of points. Make sure you get the same slope each time.

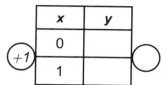

x	*y*
0	
1	

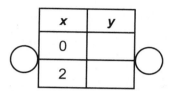

x	*y*
0	
2	

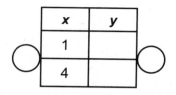

x	*y*
1	
4	

run = _____ rise = _____

slope = $\dfrac{\text{rise}}{\text{run}}$ = ──── =

run = _____ rise = _____

slope = $\dfrac{\text{rise}}{\text{run}}$ = ──── =

run = _____ rise = _____

slope = $\dfrac{\text{rise}}{\text{run}}$ = ──── =

b) Which way of finding the slope was easiest? Using x = _____ and x = _____.

2. **a)** Fill in the table using the equation. Find the slope and y-intercept.

i) $y = 3x + 2$

x	*y*
0	2
1	5

y-intercept: __2__

run = 1 rise = __5 − 2 = 3__

slope = $\dfrac{\text{rise}}{\text{run}} = \dfrac{3}{1} = 3$

ii) $y = -1.5x + 2$

x	*y*
0	
1	

y-intercept: _____

run = 1 rise = _____

slope = $\dfrac{\text{rise}}{\text{run}}$ = ──── =

iii) $y = -x - 0.5$

x	*y*
0	
1	

y-intercept: _____

run = 1 rise = _____

slope = $\dfrac{\text{rise}}{\text{run}}$ = ──── =

b) Circle the y-intercept and underline the slope in each equation. Include the sign.

c) Where can you find the y-intercept in the equation? _____

d) Where can you find the slope in the equation? _____

3. Find the slope and the y-intercept of the line from the equation.

a) $y = 4x - 5$

slope: __4__

y-intercept: __−5__

b) $y = -1.5x + 2$

slope: _____

y-intercept: _____

c) $y = -x - 0.5$

slope: _____

y-intercept: _____

d) $y = \dfrac{1}{2}x - 3$

slope: _____

y-intercept: _____

e) $y = -2x + \dfrac{1}{2}$

slope: _____

y-intercept: _____

f) $y = \dfrac{1}{2}x - \dfrac{1}{2}$

slope: _____

y-intercept: _____

To write an equation for a line, multiply x by the slope, then add the y-intercept. Write the result equal to y.

If m is the slope of a line and b is the y-intercept, then $y = mx + b$ is called the **slope-intercept form** of the line.

Examples:

Slope	y-intercept	Equation of the Line
2	3	$y = 2x + 3$
1	−2	$y = x - 2$
−5	0	$y = -5x$
1.2	0.5	$y = 1.2x + 0.5$

4. For a line with the given slope and y-intercept, write the equation of the line in slope-intercept form.

a) slope = 3, y-intercept = −3

   $\underline{\quad y = 3x - 3 \quad}$

b) slope = −3, y-intercept = 3

   $\underline{\qquad\qquad}$

c) slope = 1.4, y-intercept = −1

   $\underline{\qquad\qquad}$

d) slope = $\dfrac{1}{2}$, y-intercept = −3

   $\underline{\qquad\qquad}$

e) slope = 2, y-intercept = $-\dfrac{2}{3}$

   $\underline{\qquad\qquad}$

f) slope = $\dfrac{1}{2}$, y-intercept = $\dfrac{3}{5}$

   $\underline{\qquad\qquad}$

5. Find the slope and the y-intercept. Write the equation of the line. Hint: the y-intercept is the y-coordinate of a point that has x-coordinate equal to 0.

a) $A\,(2, -1)$, $B\,(0, -3)$

   y-intercept: *−3*

   run = *0 − 2 = −2*

   rise = *−3 − (−1) = −2*

   slope = $\dfrac{\text{rise}}{\text{run}} = \dfrac{-2}{-2} = 1$

   equation: $\underline{\quad y = x - 3 \quad}$

b) $A\,(0, 2)$, $B\,(1, 3)$

   y-intercept:

   run = $\quad - \quad =$

   rise = $\quad - \quad =$

   slope = $\dfrac{\text{rise}}{\text{run}} = \underline{\quad} =$

   equation: $\underline{\qquad\qquad}$

c) $A\,(-2, -1)$, $B\,(0, -5)$

   y-intercept:

   run = $\quad - \quad =$

   rise = $\quad - \quad =$

   slope = $\dfrac{\text{rise}}{\text{run}} = \underline{\quad} =$

   equation: $\underline{\qquad\qquad}$

d) $A\,(1, -1)$, $B\,(0, 1.5)$

   y-intercept: *1.5*

   run = *0 − 1 = −1*

   rise = *1.5 − (−1) = 2.5*

   slope = $\dfrac{\text{rise}}{\text{run}} = \dfrac{2.5}{-1} = -2.5$

   equation: $\underline{\quad y = -2.5x + 1.5 \quad}$

e) $A\,(0, -2.5)$, $B\,(1, -3.5)$

   y-intercept:

   run =

   rise =

   slope = $\dfrac{\text{rise}}{\text{run}} = \underline{\quad} =$

   equation: $\underline{\qquad\qquad}$

f) $A\,(-1, -1)$, $B\,(0, -0.5)$

   y-intercept:

   run =

   rise =

   slope = $\dfrac{\text{rise}}{\text{run}} = \underline{\quad} =$

   equation: $\underline{\qquad\qquad}$

6. Check your answers to Question 5 by substituting.

   Example: a) $y = x - 3$, $y = 2 - 3 = -1$, $A\,(2, -1)$ ✓

7. a) Extend the line to find the y-intercept. Mark two points with integer coordinates to find the slope of the line. Remember to mark the left point as *A* to have a positive run.

i)

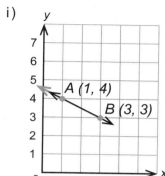

y-intercept: __4.5__

run = __3 − 1 = 2__

rise = __3 − 4 = −1__

$$\text{slope} = \frac{\text{rise}}{\text{run}} = \frac{-1}{2} = -0.5$$

ii)

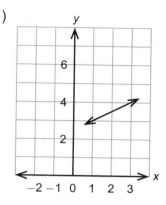

y-intercept: _____

run = _____

rise = _____

$$\text{slope} = \frac{\text{rise}}{\text{run}} = \underline{\quad} =$$

iii)

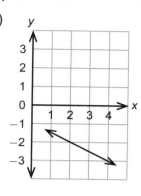

y-intercept: _____

run = _____

rise = _____

$$\text{slope} = \frac{\text{rise}}{\text{run}} = \underline{\quad} =$$

iv)

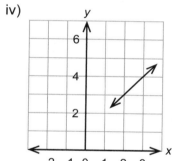

y-intercept: _____

run = _____

rise = _____

$$\text{slope} = \frac{\text{rise}}{\text{run}} = \underline{\quad} =$$

v)

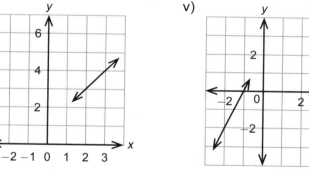

y-intercept: _____

run = _____

rise = _____

$$\text{slope} = \frac{\text{rise}}{\text{run}} = \underline{\quad} =$$

vi)

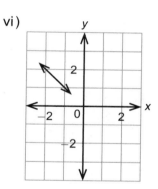

y-intercept: _____

run = _____

rise = _____

$$\text{slope} = \frac{\text{rise}}{\text{run}} = \underline{\quad} =$$

b) Write the equation for each line in part a) in slope-intercept form.

i) y = __−0.5x + 4.5__

ii) y = _____

iii) y = _____

iv) y = _____

v) y = _____

vi) y = _____

c) Which equation represents a proportional relationship between x and y? _____

53. Comparing Linear Functions

1. a) Graph both functions on the same grid. Determine which function has the greater slope and which is steeper.

   i) $y = x + 1$

   $y = 2x - 3$

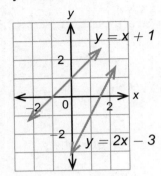

   ii) $y = 3x - 1$

   $y = x + 2$

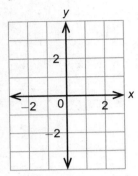

   iii) $y = 2x - 1$

   $y = x - 2$

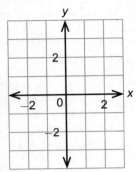

   Greater slope: <u> $y = 2x - 3$ </u>

   Steeper: <u> $y = 2x - 3$ </u>

   Greater slope: _____

   Steeper: _____

   Greater slope: _____

   Steeper: _____

   iv) $y = -x - 1$

   $y = -2x + 3$

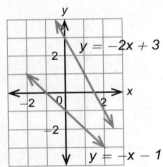

   v) $y = -3x + 1$

   $y = -2x - 2$

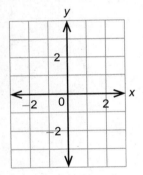

   Bonus ▶ $y = x + 1$

   $y = -3x + 1$

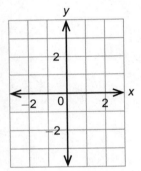

   Greater slope: <u> $y = -x - 1$ </u>

   Steeper: <u> $y = -2x + 3$ </u>

   Greater slope: _____

   Steeper: _____

   Greater slope: _____

   Steeper: _____

   b) Does a greater slope always mean a steeper slope? _____

   c) Find the absolute value of the slopes for each part in a).

   i) $|1| = 1, |2| = 2$

   ii)

   iii)

   iv) $|-1| = 1, |-2| = 2$

   v)

   Bonus ▶

   d) Does a greater absolute value slope always mean a steeper slope? _____

A greater slope does not always mean a steeper slope. You need to compare the absolute values of slopes to find out which is steeper.

Example: Line *AB* has a slope of 1 and *CD* has a slope of −3 so *AB* has a greater slope than *CD*. However, line *CD* has a steeper slope than *AB*.

Slope of *AB*: 1   Absolute value of slope of *AB*: 1

Slope of *CD*: −3   Absolute value of slope of *CD*: 3

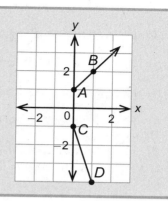

2. a) Four linear functions are represented in different ways below. Find the slope of each.

A.

x	y
−1	−4
1	2
2	5
3	8

B.

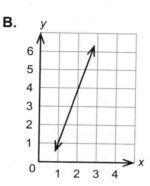

C. (−2, 0), (0, 2), (3, 5)

D. $y = -4x + 3$

b) Which two functions have the same slope? _____ and _____

c) Which function has the greatest slope? _____

d) Which function has the steepest slope? _____

3. The table shows the temperatures in the first week of May in Los Angeles, CA, at 8 a.m. and 4 p.m.

	Mon	Tue	Wed	Thu	Fri	Sat	Sun
Temperature at 8 a.m. (°F)	79	71	75	76	83	83	78
Temperature at 4 p.m. (°F)	74	71	78	84	85	77	75

a) Find the changes in temperature for each day.

	Mon	Tue	Wed	Thu	Fri	Sat	Sun
Change in Temperature	−5						

b) Which day had the greatest change in temperature? _____

c) Find the change in temperature per hour for each day.

d) Which day had the greatest change in temperature per hour? _____

e) Explain how you can use change in temperature to calculate change in temperature per hour.

_____

54. Using the Equation of a Line to Solve Word Problems

1. A train is traveling at a constant speed of 50 mi/h.

   a) Write an equation for the distance the train traveled after x hours. y = _____

   b) How far does the train travel in 3 hours? Hint: Replace x with 3. _____

   c) How far does the train travel in 4.5 hours? _____

   d) How long does it take for the train to travel 250 miles?
      Hint: Substitute y = 250 in the equation, then solve for x.

   e) How long does it take for the train to travel 425 miles?

2. To rent a pair of skates, you pay a $3 flat fee plus $2 per hour, as shown in the graph below.

   a) How much does it cost to rent a pair of skates for 1 hour? _____

   b) How much does it cost to rent a pair of skates for 3 hours? _____

   c) Julie paid $10 to rent a pair of skates. How many hours did she pay for?

      _____

   d) Find the y-intercept and the slope of the line.

      y-intercept: _____   slope = $\dfrac{\text{rise}}{\text{run}}$ = ―― =

   e) Write the equation of the line. y = _____

   f) Substitute $x = 1$ in the equation to find the cost of renting skates

      for 1 hour. _____

   g) Where do you see the flat rate in the equation? _____

   h) How you can find the answer to part b) using the equation? _____

   i) Find the answer to part c) by replacing y with 10 in the equation and solving for x.

   j) Can you use the graph as is to find the cost of renting a pair of skates for 10 hours?

      Why or why not? 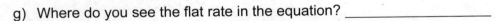 _____

   k) How could you use the equation to find the cost of renting a pair of skates for 10 hours?

      _____

3. Kim has $10 and she saves $5 every week.

a) Create a table of values for Kim's savings after x weeks.

x weeks	$y in savings
0	10
1	15
2	
3	

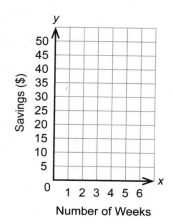

b) Plot the ordered pairs from the table of values above on the graph on the right.

c) Find the y-intercept and the slope of the line.

y-intercept: _____   slope = $\dfrac{\text{rise}}{\text{run}}$ = ____ =

d) Write the equation of the line. y = _____

e) Kim plans to buy a skateboard for $85. How many weeks must she save to buy the skateboard?

f) Did you need the graph to answer parts c), d), and e)? _____

4. Tony has a $25.00 gift card for an online role-playing game. Subscribing to the game costs $4.25 per month.

a) How much money remains on the gift card after the first month? _____

b) Fill in the table of values for his remaining money after x months.

x months	$y on gift card
0	25.00
1	20.75
2	
3	

c) For the table above, find the y-intercept and the slope of a line that goes through all points.

d) Write the equation of the line. y = _____

e) How much money remains on the gift card after 5 months? _____

55. Describing Graphs

Speed is the rate of distance traveled in a certain time.
Example: A car with a speed of 60 mi/h travels 60 miles every hour.

To find the speed, you can find the slope of the line in a
graph of distance and time, where time is the horizontal axis.

Example: run = 1 − 0 = 1 hour, and rise = 60 − 0 = 60 miles

$$\text{slope} = \frac{\text{rise}}{\text{run}} = \frac{60}{1} = 60, \text{ so the speed is 60 mi/h}$$

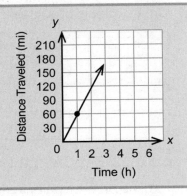

1. A group of Grade 8 students take a bike trip from their school.
   The graph shows the times and distances of their trip.

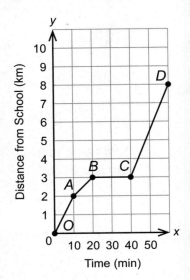

   a) How far did the students bike in 1 hour? _____

   b) Complete the table to find the slope between …

		Run (min)	Rise (km)	Slope (km/min)
i)	O and A	10 − 0 = 10	2 − 0 = 2	$\frac{\text{rise}}{\text{run}} = \frac{2}{10} = 0.2$
ii)	A and B			$\frac{\text{rise}}{\text{run}} = \underline{\quad} =$
iii)	B and C			$\frac{\text{rise}}{\text{run}} = \underline{\quad} =$
iv)	C and D			$\frac{\text{rise}}{\text{run}} = \underline{\quad} =$

   c) Which line segment has the steepest slope? _____

   d) What was the maximum speed of the group during the trip? _____

   e) The maximum speed of the group happened in between _____ minutes

      and _____ minutes.

   f) The students stopped to have a rest. Which line segment shows the rest? _____
      Hint: During the rest, the distance from the school doesn't change.

   g) What is the students' speed during the rest? _____

2. Three students run 12 km in 60 minutes.

  • Beth starts slowly and increases her speed as she warms up.

  • John runs at a constant speed.

  • Anna starts running fast, then she slows down.

a) Match the graph to the student by writing a name under each graph.

A.

Distance Traveled (km)

14 12 10 8 6 4 2 0

10 20 30 40 50

Time (min)

_____

B.

Distance Traveled (km)

14 12 10 8 6 4 2 0

10 20 30 40 50

Time (min)

_____

C.

Distance Traveled (km)

14 12 10 8 6 4 2 0

10 20 30 40 50

Time (min)

_____

b) Which graph represents a linear function? _____

3. May took a road trip to her aunt's house (500 miles away) and her grandmother's house (700 miles away). The graph shows how far from home she was during the last week.

a) How many miles did May drive in the first day? _____

b) How many days did she take to drive to her aunt's house?

   _____

c) Which days did May not drive? _____

d) How many nights did May stay at her grandmother's house?

   _____

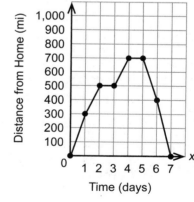

e) The nights that May didn't sleep at her relatives' homes, she stayed

in motels. How many nights did May stay in a motel? _____

f) Write a story about May's trip to describe all line segments of the graph.

_____

_____

_____

_____

4. The graph shows the number of gold medals won by the United States at each of the Summer Olympic Games from 1992 to 2012.

a) Find the slope of each line segment.

b) Which line segment has the greatest slope? _____

c) In what year did the US have the best results compared with the previous Summer Olympic year's results? _____

d) Which line segment has the smallest slope? _____

e) In what year did the US have the worst results compared with the previous Summer Olympic year's results? _____

f) Which line segment has the slope equal to 0? _____

g) In what year did the results not change from the previous Summer Olympic year? _____

5. Sam lives 900 m from his school. Today, Sam:

• walked 200 m in 4 minutes,
• then ran 600 m in 3 minutes,
• then rested for 1 minute, and
• then walked the last 100 m in 2 minutes.

a) How far did Sam go in the first 7 minutes? _____

b) How far did Sam go in the first 8 minutes? _____

c) Fill the table to find how far Sam went after t minutes. Then use the table to complete the graph at right.

Time (min)	4	7	8	10
Distance Traveled (m)	200			

d) How long does it take Sam to get to school? _____

e) Find the slope of each line segment to find Sam's speed during each part of his trip:

i)   ii)   iii)   iv)

f) In what period of time does the graph have the steepest slope? _____

56. Cumulative Review—Functions

1. Test any input number to see if the picture shows a machine. Circle the machines.

a)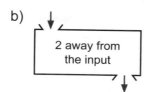

b)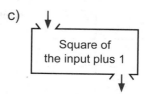

c)
Square of
the input plus 1

2. Circle the mapping diagrams that represent a function.

A. 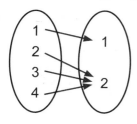 **B.** 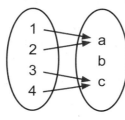 **C.** 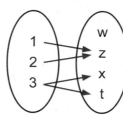 **D.**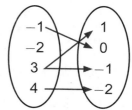

Bonus ▶ Draw a mapping diagram for the following set of ordered pairs. Does it represent a function? (1, 1), (2, 4), (3, 4), (2, 2^2), (4, 2)

3. Use the gap in the sequence to find the coefficient in the formula. Then complete the table to finish writing the formula.

a)

Input (*n*)	*n* × gap	Output
1		5
2		8
3		11

Formula: _____

Bonus ▶

Input (*n*)	*n* × gap	Output
1		0
2		−2
3		−4

Formula: _____

4. Match the graph to the equation.

A. 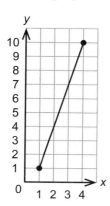   **B.** 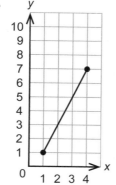   **C.**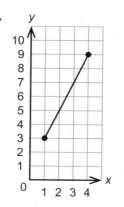

a) $y = 2x + 1$ _____   b) $y = 3x − 2$ _____   c) $y = 2x − 1$ _____

5. A ship is traveling across the ocean at a constant speed of 30 mi/h.

a) Create a table of values for the distance the ship traveled after t hours.

t (hours)	Distance Traveled (mi)
1	
2	
3	

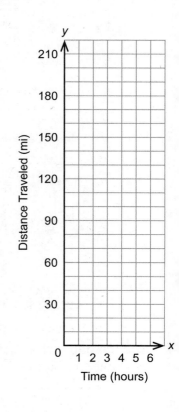

b) Write the ordered pairs from the above table of values. Then plot the points on the graph on the right.

c) Join the points on the graph with a straight line. If the ship

traveled 3.5 hours, about how far would it go? _____

d) About how many hours would it take the ship to travel 195 miles?

Extend the line to find out. _____

e) Find the slope of the line using the table in part a). _____

f) Write the equation of the line. y = _____

g) Answer parts c) and d) using the equation of the line.

h) Can you use the graph to find exactly how long it takes to go 160 miles? _____

i) Use the equation of the line to find exactly how long it takes to go 160 miles.

6. Kevin left his home to walk to school 500 m away. After a while, he realized he forgot something. The graph shows how far he was from home.

a) How far did Kevin walk before he noticed he forgot something?

_____

b) How many minutes did it take to walk back home? _____

c) How many minutes was Kevin at home again? _____

d) Find the slope of all four line segments.

e) When does Kevin walk faster toward the school: when he first

leaves home or after he gets what he forgot? _____

f) Write a story to describe the graph.

57. Square Roots

$6 \times 6 = 36$, so $6^2 = 36$. We say the **square** of 6 is 36.

Examples: $\left(\dfrac{2}{7}\right)^2 = \dfrac{2}{7} \times \dfrac{2}{7} = \dfrac{4}{49}$ $0.5^2 = 0.5 \times 0.5 = 0.25$

1. Evaluate the power.

a) $7^2 = \underline{\quad 49 \quad}$ b) $9^2 = \underline{\qquad}$ c) $10^2 = \underline{\qquad}$ d) $8^2 = \underline{\qquad}$

e) $\left(\dfrac{1}{4}\right)^2 = \underline{\quad}$ f) $\left(\dfrac{3}{10}\right)^2 = \underline{\quad}$ g) $0.2^2 = \underline{\qquad}$ h) $1.1^2 = \underline{\qquad}$

The **square root** of 25 is 5 because $5^2 = 25$. We write $\sqrt{25} = 5$.

Examples: $\sqrt{\dfrac{9}{16}} = \dfrac{3}{4}$ because $\left(\dfrac{3}{4}\right)^2 = \dfrac{9}{16}$ $\sqrt{0.01} = 0.1$ because $(0.1)^2 = 0.01$

2. Find the square root.

a) $\sqrt{49} = \underline{\quad 7 \quad}$ b) $\sqrt{16} = \underline{\qquad}$ c) $\sqrt{9} = \underline{\qquad}$ d) $\sqrt{36} = \underline{\qquad}$

e) $\sqrt{1} = \underline{\qquad}$ f) $\sqrt{100} = \underline{\qquad}$ g) $\sqrt{81} = \underline{\qquad}$ h) $\sqrt{64} = \underline{\qquad}$

i) $\sqrt{\dfrac{4}{9}} = \underline{\quad}$ j) $\sqrt{\dfrac{49}{100}} = \underline{\quad}$ k) $\sqrt{0.09} = \underline{\qquad}$ l) $\sqrt{1.44} = \underline{\qquad}$

3. Evaluate the square roots and then multiply, divide, add, or subtract.

a) $\sqrt{1} + \sqrt{64}$ b) $\sqrt{81} - \sqrt{25}$ c) $\sqrt{36} \div \sqrt{4}$ d) $\sqrt{25} + \sqrt{16} \times \sqrt{9}$

$= 1 + 8$

$= 9$

4. Evaluate both expressions. Then write $=$ or $\neq$ in the box.

a) $\sqrt{4 \times 9}$ $\boxed{=}$ $\sqrt{4} \times \sqrt{9}$

    $= \sqrt{36}$ $= 2 \times 3$

    $= 6$ $= 6$

b) $\sqrt{9 + 16}$ $\boxed{}$ $\sqrt{9} + \sqrt{16}$

c) $\sqrt{169 - 25}$ $\boxed{}$ $\sqrt{169} - \sqrt{25}$

d) $\sqrt{100 \div 4}$ $\boxed{}$ $\sqrt{100} \div \sqrt{4}$

5. a) Evaluate the powers.

   i) $5^2 =$ _____

   $(-5)^2 =$ _____

   ii) $11^2 =$ _____

   $(-11)^2 =$ _____

   iii) $12^2 =$ _____

   $(-12)^2 =$ _____

   iv) $3^2 =$ _____

   $(-3)^2 =$ _____

   b) Write "positive" or "negative."

   i) The square of a positive number is a _____ number.

   ii) The square of a negative number is a _____ number.

> Every positive number has a positive square root and a negative square root.
>
> Example: $(4)^2 = 16$ and $(-4)^2 = 16$, so 4 and -4 are square roots of 16.

6. Write two square roots of the number.

   a) 81

   __9__ and __−9__

   b) 49

   _____ and _____

   c) 25

   _____ and _____

   d) 0.16

   _____ and _____

7. Write two solutions for the equation.

   a) $x^2 = 1$

   $x =$ __1__ and __−1__

   b) $x^2 = 9$

   $x =$ ____ and _____

   c) $x^2 = 121$

   $x =$ ____ and _____

   d) $x^2 = 0.04$

   $x =$ ____ and _____

> The equation $x^2 = 81$ has two solutions: $x = 9$ and $x = -9$. We write $x = \pm 9$ to indicate that the solution can be positive or negative.
>
> $x^2 = 81$
>
> $x = 9$ and $x = -9$
>
> $x = \pm 9$
>
> Check: $x^2 = 81$
>
> $(9)^2 = 81$ ✓
>
> $(-9)^2 = 81$ ✓

8. Solve the equation.

   a) $x^2 = 144$

   $x = 12$ and $x = -12$

   $x = \pm 12$

   b) $x^2 = 9$

   c) $x^2 = \dfrac{36}{49}$

   d) $x^2 = 0.09$

   e) $x^2 + 5 = 41$

   f) $4x^2 - 6 = 10$

   g) $x^2 + \dfrac{1}{2} = \dfrac{3}{4}$

   Bonus ▶ $\dfrac{2}{3}x^2 - 15 = 1\dfrac{2}{3}$

9. Jayden's garden is a square. The area is 49 ft². What is the perimeter?

10. A square painting has an area of 36 in². Kathy says the length of one side could be 6 inches or −6 inches. What is Kathy's mistake?

The **principal square root** of a number is the positive square root of the number. We write $\sqrt{36} = 6$.

To indicate the negative square root, we write $-\sqrt{36} = -6$.

To indicate both the positive and negative square roots, we write $\pm\sqrt{36} = \pm 6$.

11. Evaluate.

a) $-\sqrt{100} = \underline{\quad -10 \quad}$ 　　 b) $\pm\sqrt{121} = \underline{\qquad}$ 　　 c) $\sqrt{0.0144} = \underline{\qquad}$ 　　 d) $\pm\sqrt{1} = \underline{\qquad}$

e) $\pm\sqrt{30-5}$

　　$= \pm\sqrt{25}$

　　$= \pm 5$

f) $-\sqrt{81} - \sqrt{1}$ 　　 g) $\pm\sqrt{29+7}$ 　　 h) $\sqrt{36} + \sqrt{1} - \sqrt{25}$

Since the solution to the equation $x^2 = 49$ can be positive or negative, we write $x = \pm\sqrt{49} = \pm 7$.

12. Solve the equation.

a) $x^2 = 4$

　　$x = \pm\sqrt{4}$

　　$x = \pm 2$

b) $x^2 = 25$ 　　 c) $x^2 = \dfrac{1}{100}$ 　　 d) $x^2 = 1.44$

13. a) Evaluate using the standard order of operations.

i) $\left(\sqrt{16}\right)^2$

　　$= (4)^2$

　　$= 16$

ii) $\left(\sqrt{100}\right)^2$ 　　 iii) $\left(\sqrt{64}\right)^2$ 　　 iv) $\left(\sqrt{81}\right)^2$

b) What do you notice about your answers to part a)?

14. a) To solve for x, square both sides of the equation. Group any like terms first.

i) $\sqrt{x} = 8$

　　$\left(\sqrt{x}\right)^2 = 8^2$

　　$x = 64$

ii) $\sqrt{x} = \dfrac{2}{5}$ 　　 iii) $5 - 2 = \sqrt{x}$ 　　 **Bonus ▶** $8 = \sqrt{x} + 7$

b) Check your answers to part a).

i) $\sqrt{x} = 8$

　　$\sqrt{64} = 8$ ✓

ii) 　　 iii) 　　 **Bonus ▶**

58. Areas of Triangles and Parallelograms

REMINDER: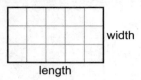

Area of a rectangle = length × width

= 5 × 3

= 15 square units

Area of a right triangle = area of rectangle ÷ 2

= 5 × 3 ÷ 2

= 7.5 square units

1. Find the area of the right triangles.

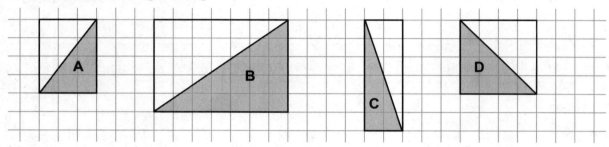

Area of A = _____ × _____ ÷ 2

= _____ square units

Area of B = _____ × _____ ÷ 2

= _____ square units

Area of C = _____ × _____ ÷ 2

= _____ square units

Area of D = _____ × _____ ÷ 2

= _____ square units

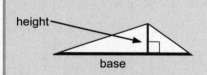  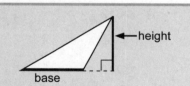

The height of a triangle is the length of a perpendicular line segment from the vertex to the base.

2. Use a ruler to draw the height of the triangle.

a)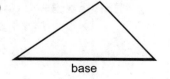

b)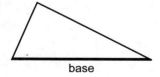

c)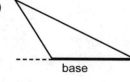

d)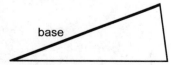

e)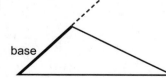

f)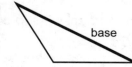

The area of an acute triangle is one half the area of a rectangle with the same base and height.

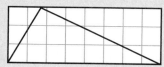 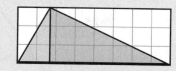

Area of triangle = base × height ÷ 2
= 8 × 3 ÷ 2
= 12 square units

3. Count squares to find the base and height. Then use the formula to find the area of the acute triangle.

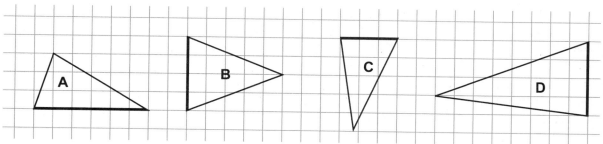

Area of A = _____ × _____ ÷ 2

= _____ square units

Area of C = _____ × _____ ÷ 2

= _____ square units

Area of B = _____ × _____ ÷ 2

= _____ square units

Area of D = _____ × _____ ÷ 2

= _____ square units

The area of an obtuse triangle is one half the area of a rectangle with the same base and height.

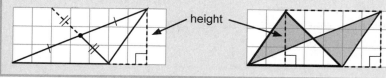

Area of triangle = base × height ÷ 2
= 5 × 3 ÷ 2
= 7.5 square units

4. Count squares to find the base and height. Then use the formula to find the area of the obtuse triangle.

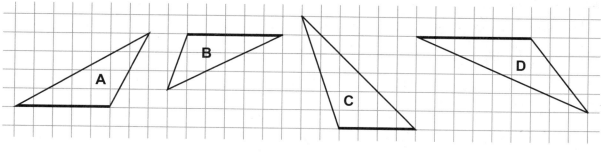

Area of A = _____ × _____ ÷ 2

= _____ square units

Area of C = _____ × _____ ÷ 2

= _____ square units

Area of B = _____ × _____ ÷ 2

= _____ square units

Area of D = _____ × _____ ÷ 2

= _____ square units

5. The triangles are congruent. Measure the base and height of each triangle to the nearest tenth of a centimeter. Then find the area.

A.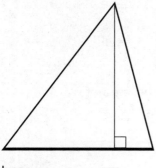

base = _____ cm

height = _____ cm

Area = _____ × _____ ÷ 2

= _____ cm²

B.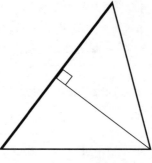

base = _____ cm

height = _____ cm

Area = _____ × _____ ÷ 2

= _____ cm²

6. a) What do you notice about your answers to Question 5?

b) Does the area change if you choose a different side of the triangle to be the base?

c) Draw an obtuse triangle and find the area using different sides as the base. The area should be the same. If not, find your mistake.

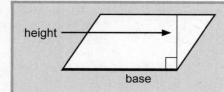

height ——

base

The height of a parallelogram is the length of a perpendicular line segment from the base to the opposite side.

7. Sketch a line to show the height of the parallelogram for the given base.

A

base

B

C

D

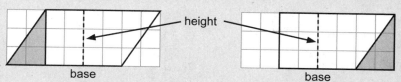

The area of a parallelogram is the same as the area of a rectangle with the same base and height.

height

base   base

Area of parallelogram
= base × height
= 6 × 3
= 18 square units

8. Mark and measure the height and base to the nearest tenth of a centimeter.
Then find the area.

a)
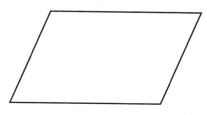

Area = _____ cm × _____ cm

= _____ cm²

b)
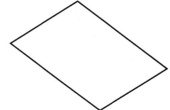

Area = _____ cm × _____ cm

= _____ cm²

9. Find the area of parallelogram *ABCD* in two different ways.
First use *AB* as the base. Then use *BC* as the base.
How do the answers compare? Why?

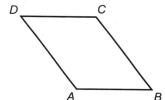

10. Find the area of the trapezoid. Hint: Add the areas of the parallelogram and triangle.

a)
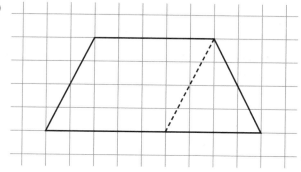

Area of
parallelogram = _____ × _____ = _____

Area of
triangle = _____ × _____ ÷ 2 = _____

Area of
trapezoid = _____ + _____ = _____ units²

b)

Area of
parallelogram = _____ × _____ = _____

Area of
triangle = _____ × _____ ÷ 2 = _____

Area of
trapezoid = _____ + _____ = _____ units²

59. Introduction to the Pythagorean Theorem

1. Find the area of the right triangle.

a)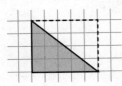

Area = __20__ ÷ 2 = __10__

b)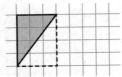

Area = _____ ÷ 2 = _____

c)

Area = _____ ÷ 2 = _____

2. Find the area of each square by finding the area of 4 right triangles and what is left.

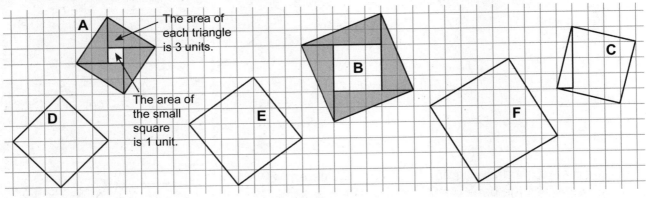

The area of each triangle is 3 units.

The area of the small square is 1 unit.

Area of A = 4 × __3__ + __1__ = __13__

3. What is the side length of square E in Question 2? How do you know?

4. Find the side length of each square.

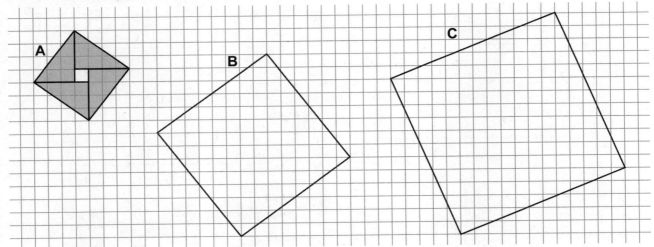

Side length of A

$= \sqrt{4 \times 6 + 1}$

$= \sqrt{25} = 5$

Side length of B

$= \sqrt{4 \times \underline{} + \underline{}}$

$= \sqrt{\underline{}} = \underline{}$

Side length of C

$= \sqrt{4 \times \underline{} + \underline{}}$

$= \sqrt{\underline{}} = \underline{}$

5. a) Find the area of the squares with side lengths *a*, *b*, and *c*. Write your answers in the table. Leave the last column empty.

i)
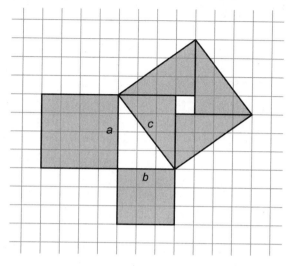

ii)
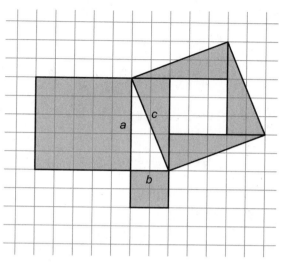

iii)
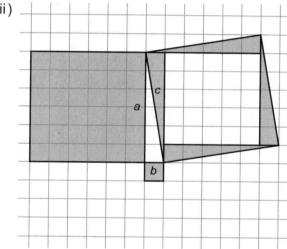

iv)
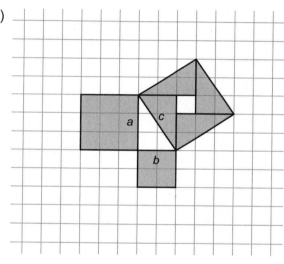

	a^2	b^2	c^2	$a^2 + b^2$
i)	$4 \times 4 = 16$	$3 \times 3 = 9$	$4 \times 6 + 1 = 25$	
ii)				
iii)				
iv)				

b) For each row in the table, calculate the value of $a^2 + b^2$. Fill in the last column.

c) Compare your answers to the last two columns: c^2 and $a^2 + b^2$. Make a conjecture: If *c* is the side opposite the right angle in a right triangle with sides *a*, *b*, *c*,

then _____.

6. Check your conjecture from Question 5.c) by measuring the length of each side of the right triangle to the nearest tenth of a centimeter.

a)

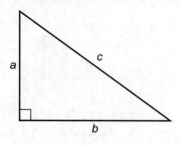

$a =$ _____ $b =$ _____ $c =$ _____

$a^2 =$ _____ $b^2 =$ _____ $c^2 =$ _____

$a^2 + b^2 =$ _____

b)

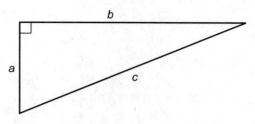

$a =$ _____ $b =$ _____ $c =$ _____

$a^2 =$ _____ $b^2 =$ _____ $c^2 =$ _____

$a^2 + b^2 =$ _____

7. Use $c^2 = a^2 + b^2$ to find the length of c.

a)

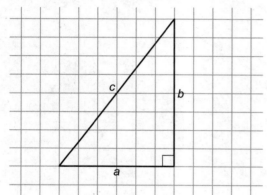

$c^2 = a^2 + b^2$

$= $ _____^{2} $+$ _____^{2}

$= $ _____ $+$ _____

$= $ _____

$c = \sqrt{\rule{1.5cm}{0pt}} = $ _____

b)

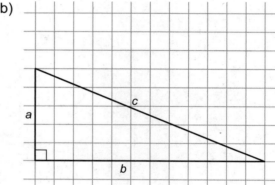

$c^2 = a^2 + b^2$

$= $ _____^{2} $+$ _____^{2}

$= $ _____ $+$ _____

$= $ _____

$c = \sqrt{\rule{1.5cm}{0pt}} = $ _____

8. The sides that are not opposite the right angle in a right triangle are given. Find the length of the side opposite the right angle.

a) 8, 15

b) 9, 12

60. The Pythagorean Theorem

<table>
<tr><td>In a right triangle, the side opposite the right angle is called the **hypotenuse**.</td><td>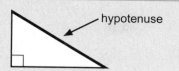</td></tr>
</table>

1. Mark the hypotenuse of the triangle with a thick line.

a)   b)   c) 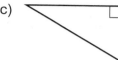   d)

Pythagorean Theorem

In a right triangle, the hypotenuse squared is the sum of the squares of the other two sides.

If the hypotenuse is labeled c, and the other sides are labeled a and b, then $c^2 = a^2 + b^2$.

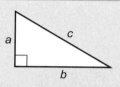

$$c^2 = a^2 + b^2$$

2. Use the Pythagorean Theorem to write an equation for the triangle.

a) 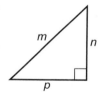   b) 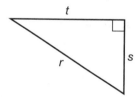   c)   d)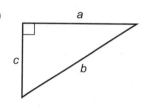

_____   _____   _____   _____

3. Use the Pythagorean Theorem to find the hypotenuse.

a) 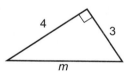   b) 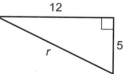   c)   d)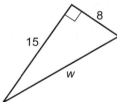

$\underline{\quad m^2 = 4^2 + 3^2 \quad}$

$\underline{\quad m^2 = 16 + 9 \quad}$

$\underline{\quad m^2 = 25 \quad}$

$\underline{\quad m = \sqrt{25} = 5 \quad}$

You can use the Pythagorean Theorem to find any side of a right triangle if two sides are given.

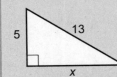

$5^2 + x^2 = 13^2$

$25 + x^2 = 169$

$x^2 = 169 - 25 = 144$

so $x = \sqrt{144} = 12$

4. Use the Pythagorean Theorem to write an equation for the triangle. Then find the missing side.

a) 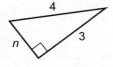   b)   c)   d)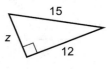

$n^2 + 3^2 = 4^2$ _____   _____   _____

$n^2 + 9 = 16$ _____   _____   _____

$n^2 = 16 - 9 = 7$ _____   _____   _____

$n = \sqrt{7}$ _____   _____   _____

5. Find the missing side of the triangle using the Pythagorean Theorem.

a) 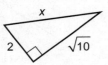   b)   c)   d)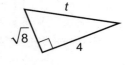

$2^2 + \left(\sqrt{10}\right)^2 = x^2$ _____   _____   _____

$4 + 10 = x^2$ _____   _____   _____

$14 = x^2$ _____   _____   _____

$x = \sqrt{14}$ _____   _____   _____

$x \approx 3.7$ _____   _____   _____

6. Find the missing side of the triangle.

a) 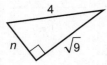   b)   c)    d)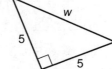

61. Proving the Pythagorean Theorem

1. Look at Figure 1.

Figure 1

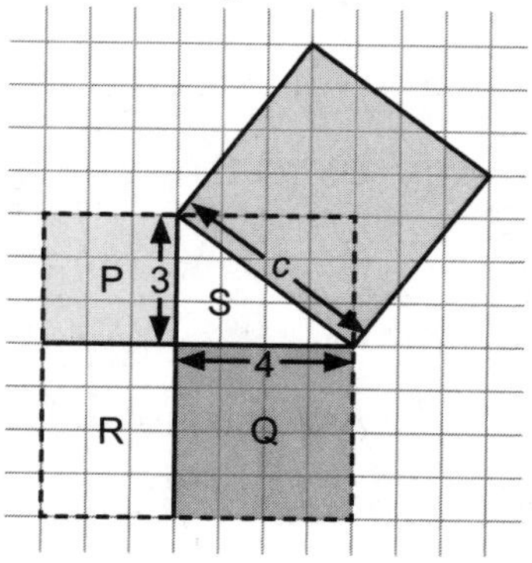

a) What is the width of square P? _____

b) What is the width of square Q? _____

c) Do the rectangles R and S have the same area? _____

How do you know? _____

d) Fill in the blanks to write an expression for each area.

Area of square P: _____²   Area of square Q: _____²

Area of rectangle R: _____ × _____

Area of rectangle S: _____ × _____

Area of the square with the dashed outline: _____

2. Look at Figure 2.

Figure 2

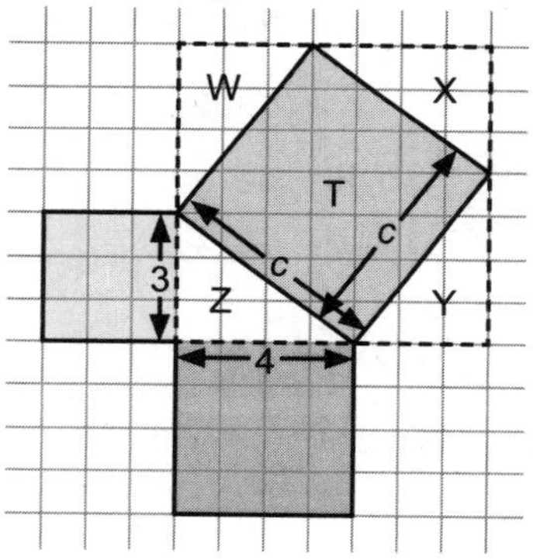

a) Triangles Z and X make a rectangle. What is its area? _____ × _____

b) Triangles W and Y make a rectangle. What is its area? _____ × _____

c) Write an expression for the length and width of square T. _____

d) Write an expression for the area of square T. _____²

e) Use your answers in parts a), b), and d) to write an expression for the area of the square with the dashed outline.

_____

3. a) In Figure 1, count the squares to find the width and length of the square with the dashed outline.   width = _____   length = _____

b) In Figure 2, count the squares to find the width and length of the square with the dashed outline.   width = _____   length = _____

c) What can you say about the areas of the dash-outlined squares in Figure 1 and Figure 2? _____

d) Use your answers to Questions 2.e) and 1.d) to write an equation.

_____

e) In the equation above, cross out parts that are the same on both sides to find an equation for c^2. _____

4. Look at Figure 3.

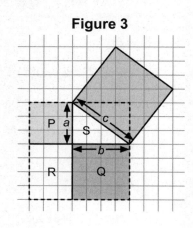

Figure 3

a) Write an expression for the width of square P. _____

b) Write an expression for the width of square Q. _____

c) Do rectangles R and S have the same area? _____

How do you know? _____

d) Fill in the blanks to write an expression for each area.

Area of square P: _____²   Area of square Q: _____²

Area of rectangle R: _____ × _____

Area of rectangle S: _____ × _____

Area of the square with the dashed outline: _____

5. Look at Figure 4.

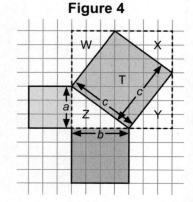

Figure 4

a) Triangles Z and X make a rectangle. Write an expression

for the area of the rectangle. _____ × _____

b) Triangles Y and W make a rectangle. Write an expression

for the area of the rectangle. _____ × _____

c) Write an expression for the length and width of square T. _____

d) Write an expression for the area of square T. _____²

e) Use your answers in parts a), b), and d) to write an expression
for the area of the square with the dashed outline.

_____

6. a) For Figure 3, write an expression for the width and length of the square with the

dashed outline.   width = _____   length = _____

b) For Figure 4, write an expression for the width and length of the square with the

dashed outline.   width = _____   length = _____

c) What can be said about the areas of the dash-outlined squares in Figure 3 and

Figure 4? _____

d) Use your answers to Questions 5.e) and 4.d) to write an equation.

_____

e) In the equation above, cross out parts that are the same on both sides to find

an equation for c^2. _____

62. Pythagorean Theorem Word Problems

1. Tom lets out 80 m of string while flying his kite.
   When he is 50 m away from Mary, the kite is directly above Mary.
   How high is the kite above Mary?

   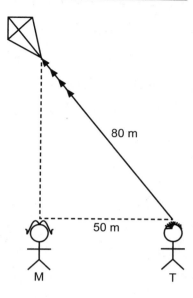

2. Ava wants to buy a new television. She has space for a TV screen
   that is 43.6 inches wide and 24.5 inches tall. TVs are sold using one
   measurement: the length of a diagonal line from one corner of the
   screen to the opposite corner. What is the largest TV screen that
   Ava can buy?

   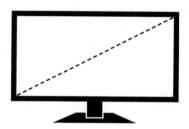

3. Sam must buy fencing to go around a field that is in the shape of a
   right triangle, as shown on the right. Find the length of fencing needed,
   rounded to the nearest meter.

   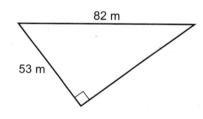

4. Mike is using a ladder that extends to reach a height of 32 feet up
   a wall. For safety, he must place the base of the ladder 1 foot away
   from the wall for every 4 feet in height.

   a) Label 32 feet up the wall in the diagram. The diagram is not to scale.

   b) How far should the base of the ladder be from the wall?
      Label this distance on the diagram.

   c) Find the length of the ladder to the nearest foot. Label the diagram.

   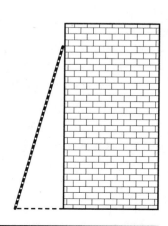

5. The isosceles triangle has equal sides each 8 cm long and a base 10 cm long.

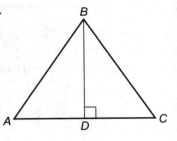

   a) Find the length of *AD*.

   b) Find the height of the triangle to the nearest tenth of a centimeter.

   c) Find the approximate area of the triangle.

6. Find the height of the parallelogram shown on the right.

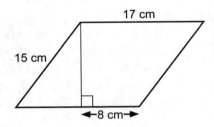

7. Marta usually walks to school by walking 2 km east, and then 1 km north. On Monday, Marta took a shortcut by walking through a park on a diagonal. To the nearest meter, how much shorter is her trip when she takes the shortcut?

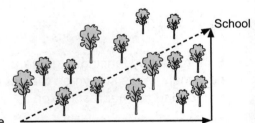

8. The bases on a baseball diamond are 90 feet apart.

   a) If the catcher is at home plate and wants to throw the ball to second base, how far must the catcher throw the ball? Round your answer to the nearest tenth of a foot.

   b) The pitcher pitches from a point 60.5 feet from home plate on a direct line from home plate to second base. Is the pitcher closer to home plate or second base? Explain.

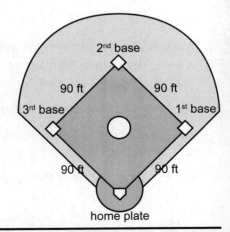

JUMP Math Accumula

63. More Pythagorean Theorem Word Problems

📒 Answer all problems in your notebook.

1. A bridge needs to be built across a marsh. The distance across the marsh is too difficult to measure. Instead, three measurements around the marsh are taken. Find the length of the bridge to the nearest meter by following these steps:

   a) In △BCD, find the length of BC.

   b) In △ACB, find the length of AC.

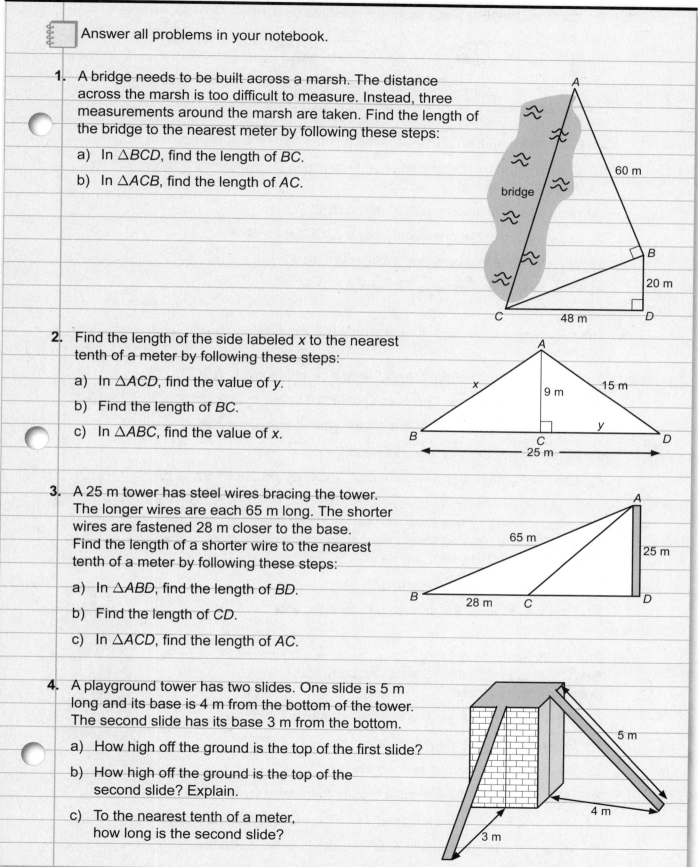

2. Find the length of the side labeled x to the nearest tenth of a meter by following these steps:

   a) In △ACD, find the value of y.

   b) Find the length of BC.

   c) In △ABC, find the value of x.

3. A 25 m tower has steel wires bracing the tower. The longer wires are each 65 m long. The shorter wires are fastened 28 m closer to the base. Find the length of a shorter wire to the nearest tenth of a meter by following these steps:

   a) In △ABD, find the length of BD.

   b) Find the length of CD.

   c) In △ACD, find the length of AC.

4. A playground tower has two slides. One slide is 5 m long and its base is 4 m from the bottom of the tower. The second slide has its base 3 m from the bottom.

   a) How high off the ground is the top of the first slide?

   b) How high off the ground is the top of the second slide? Explain.

   c) To the nearest tenth of a meter, how long is the second slide?

5. The same rectangular prism is shown twice, below.

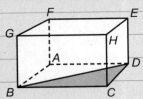 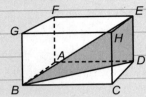

    a) *BD* is a diagonal on the base of the prism. What type of triangle is △BCD?

    b) *BE* is a diagonal from the base of the prism to the diagonally opposite corner. What type of triangle is △BDE?

    c) What side is shared by △BCD and △BDE?

    d) Draw a copy of the prism and sketch △ABC and △ACF.

    e) What types of triangles are △ABC and △ACF?

    f) What side is shared by △ABC and △ACF?

6. The rectangular prism shown on the right is 3 cm wide, 4 cm long, and 12 cm tall.

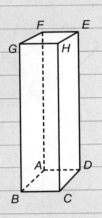

    a) Draw the diagonal from *B* to *D*. What type of triangle is △BCD?

    b) Use the Pythagorean Theorem and △BCD to find the length of *BD*.

    c) Draw the diagonal from *B* to *E*. What type of triangle is △BDE?

    d) What side do the two triangles share?

    e) Use the Pythagorean Theorem and △BDE to find the length of *BE*.

7. A storage room is 12 feet wide, 16 feet long, and 8 feet tall. A spider spins a web that has one strand from a top corner of the room to the diagonally opposite bottom corner.

    a) Draw a diagram of the room.

    b) Find the length of the strand spun by the spider.

8. Ben's suitcase is 60 cm long, 20 cm wide, and 80 cm tall. Ben wants to fit the tallest Statue of Liberty souvenir possible in his suitcase.

    a) Draw a diagonal from *A* to *C*. What shape is △ABC?

    b) Draw a diagonal from *A* to *F*. What shape is △ACF?

    c) What side is shared by the two triangles?

    d) Use △ABC to find the length of *AC* to the nearest tenth of a centimeter.

    e) Use △ACF to find the length of *AF* to the nearest tenth of a centimeter.

    f) What is the tallest souvenir that Ben can fit in his suitcase?